LIMITED EDITION

WATCHES

150 EXCLUSIVE MODERN DESIGNS

STEVEN HUYTON

Schiffer Publishing Ltd®

4880 Lower Valley Road • Atglen, PA 19310

"Schiffer," "Schiffer Publishing, Ltd.," and the pen and inkwell logo are registered trademarks of Schiffer Publishing, Ltd.

Library of Congress Control Number: 2016941196

Designed by Justin Watkinson
Cover design by Molly Shields
Type set in Akzidenz-Grotesk/Minion Pro
ISBN: 978-0-7643-5164-8
Printed in China

Published by Schiffer Publishing, Ltd.
4880 Lower Valley Road
Atglen, PA 19310
Phone: (610) 593-1777; Fax: (610) 593-2002
E-mail: Info@schifferbooks.com
Web: www.schifferbooks.com

Other Schiffer Books on Related Subjects:
A. Lange & Söhne® Highlights, ISBN: 978-0-7643-4361-2
Breitling Highlights, ISBN: 978-0-7643-4211-0
Rolex Wristwatches: An Unauthorized History, ISBN: 978-0-7643-2437-6

For our complete selection of fine books on this and related subjects, please visit our website at www.schifferbooks.com. You may also write for a free catalog.

Schiffer Publishing's titles are available at special discounts for bulk purchases for sales promotions or premiums. Special editions, including personalized covers, corporate imprints, and excerpts, can be created in large quantities for special needs. For more information, contact the publisher.

We are always looking for people to write books on new and related subjects. If you have an idea for a book, please contact us at proposals@schifferbooks.com.

Foreword

With this book I want to illustrate a diverse range of designs from some of the most famous watchmakers in the industry and smaller more exclusive artisans. There will be 150 different timepieces featured, each with two beautiful images presenting their finest creations. All of the watches showcased are limited production editions and in many instances unique pieces. Essentially, this makes them very exclusive and highly sought after. Some of these timepieces are incredibly expensive, but others (relatively speaking) are more attainable. The inclusion of these watches is not based on brand status or price, but purely on merit. Ultimately, it is a celebration of creative design and exceptional craftsmanship within the industry. It is also pertinent to mention this is not a review book and the timepieces are not in order of preference.

Since childhood, I have had a keen interest in clocks and wristwatches. As I approached my adult years this passion developed from a hobby into a career. Twenty years ago there did not seem much choice and most timepieces looked very similar in appearance; they were treated purely as a functional device and not as a collectible. In the 1970s, mechanical watches fell out of favor in preference of new quartz models. Fortunately, over the last decade the watch industry is going through a new and exciting renaissance period.

In today's market watchmakers are becoming a lot more experimental, distinguishing themselves from their contemporaries. For example, brands are using materials (as well as platinum, gold, silver, and steel) like sapphire crystal, carbon composites, lightweight alloys (titanium, magnesium, zirconium, aluminium, etc.), bronze, meteorite, and even concrete. There is even a timepiece featured in this book made entirely from wood, including the mechanical movement. This just shows the lengths these ateliers will go to create something completely unique.

Originally I started writing about timepieces because I was stimulated by many of the designs. In the past watch designs have been primarily based on pocket watches and the historic clock. Certainly this is still a creative source for some watchmakers, but a lot are finding inspiration elsewhere, such as in architecture, automobiles, and fine art. Whereas a few years ago a watch with a 40 mm diameter would have been considered large, these days there are many models in excess of 50 mm. In fact, the largest timepiece featured in this book has a case size measuring 106 mm × 62 mm × 23 mm.

Even though mechanical watch technology has not changed in 250 years, modern watchmakers are striving to improve accuracy by introducing different materials like silicon, titanium, and alloys. This not only makes the caliber a lot more lightweight, but also increases the durability. To offer the best content I have included a broad spectrum of movements ranging from highly complicated to the more humble seventeen-jewel manual winding mechanism. They all showcase exceptional traditional skills like engraving, polishing, chamfering, and hand decoration.

Although I have written a certain amount of text about each watch, I did not want it to detract from the beautiful images. The concept was to produce a visual extravaganza with a brief description of each timepiece that will introduce the watchmaker and supply a moderate amount of technical information. Hopefully you enjoy reading this book as much as I have researching, writing, and collating this information.

Phoenix 10.3, 30. Switzerland

A. Favre & Fils Phoenix 10.3

A. Favre & Fils is a traditional watchmaker in Geneva, Switzerland. The Phoenix 10.3 is the company's third and most impressive model. With a classical 18-karat white gold case measuring 41 mm × 10.20 mm, the watch is designed to make a subtle statement. What makes this timepiece so attractive is the sublime multi-layered dial delicately exposing elements of the mechanism. Other features include a transparent sapphire crystal chapter ring with vibrant blue numerals and stylish skeletonized hour/minute hands. Powering the watch is an in-house-developed twin barrel 65-jewel manual winding mechanical movement.

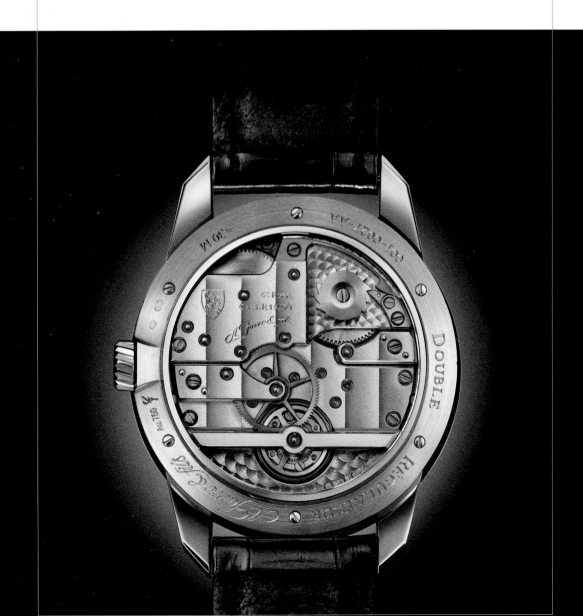

A. LANGE & SÖHNE

GLASHÜTTE I/SA

AB AUF

52

7

MADE IN GERMANY

Zeitwerk Minute Repeater, . Germany

A. Lange & Söhne
Zeitwerk Minute Repeater

A. Lange & Söhne is a German watchmaker of the highest level. Their sensational Zeitwerk Minute Repeater is the first watch featuring a striking mechanism that sounds the hours and minutes at ten-minute intervals. Dimensionally the watch exudes classical proportions and has an 18-karat white gold case measuring 42 mm × 14.1 mm. What makes this timepiece so extraordinary is the meticulous attention to detail. The dial displays hours, minutes, seconds, day/date, and a retrograde power reserve indication. Powering the watch is a sophisticated manual winding manufacture calibre that oscillates at a frequency of 18,000 vibrations per hour.

Tourbillon Chiming
Jump Hour, 10 a
year. Switzerland

AkriviA Tourbillon Chiming Jump Hour

AkriviA is a small independent Swiss watchmaker owned and operated by Rexhep Rexhepi. The Tourbillon Chiming Jump Hour is the company's third and latest model. Dimensionally the watch is classically proportioned and has a brushed steel case measuring 43 mm × 12.90 mm. What makes this timepiece so striking is the way time is actually presented: jumping hours are displayed via a small window and minutes by a bespoke central hand. Other features include a minimalistic chapter ring and aperture (located at six o'clock) showcasing the majestic rotating tourbillon carriage. Beneath the luxurious exterior lies a highly accomplished 26-jewel mechanical manual winding movement. This amazing watch is limited to only ten pieces and is priced at $206,000.

Kamar, 30. Switzerland

Andersen Genève Kamar

Andersen Genève is a small independent company owned by distinguished watchmaker Sven Andersen. The Kamar was originally released in 2011, and was available in many interesting versions. Dimensionally the timepiece displays generous proportions and has an exquisite 18-Karat white gold case measuring 45 mm × 11 mm. What makes this watch special is the sensational hand-decorated gold dial with contrasting large silver Arabic numerals. Other refined features include delicate skeletonized hour/minute hands and a large round aperture showcasing a mother of pearl moon phase indication. At the heart of the watch is a Swiss-made 28-jewel mechanical self-winding movement.

Papillon d'Or, 8. Switzerland

Andreas Strehler Papillon d'Or

Andreas Strehler describes himself as a watchmaker and not a brand. The Papillon d'Or perfectly illustrates his incredible skills and craftsmanship. Dimensionally the watch has a generous-size palladium white gold cushion-shaped case measuring 47.20 mm × 41 mm × 10 mm. What makes this watch so attractive is the distinctive open-worked three-dimensional dial. Other features include an offset sub dial (located at three o'clock) displaying hours/minutes and ergonomic lugs. Powering the watch is a 27-jewel Swiss-made bespoke mechanical manual winding movement. This caliber is composed of 162 individual parts and oscillates at a frequency of 21,600 vibrations per hour.

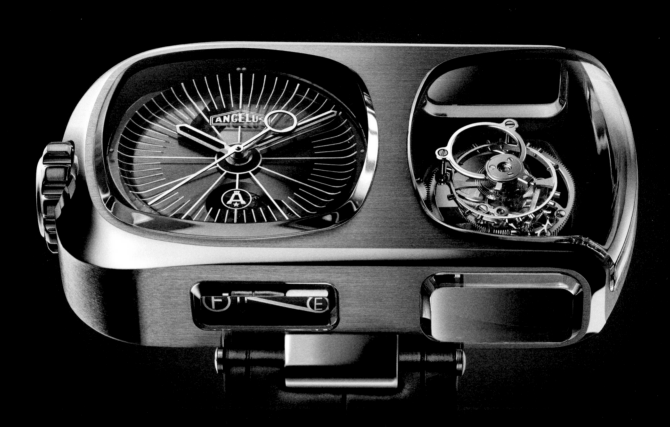

Angelus U10 Tourbillon Lumière

Angelus is a historic watchmaker established by brothers Albert and Gustav Stolz in 1891. In 2011, La Joux-Perret SA revived the brand and they unveiled a timepiece called the U10 Tourbillon Lumière. With a rectangular stainless steel case measuring 62.75 mm × 38 mm × 15 mm, the watch is designed to make a bold statement. What makes this timepiece so extraordinary is the two sapphire windows displaying the time and a seemingly floating tourbillon. At the heart of the watch is an in-house-manufactured mechanical manual winding movement containing 38 jewels. The timepiece is limited to twenty-five pieces worldwide and is priced at $102,773.

Polyphemos, 10. Switzerland

Angular Momentum
Polyphemos

Angular Momentum is a small Swiss brand that specializes in the manufacture of custom-made watches. The company is the brainchild of Martin Pauli, and the Polyphemos is a perfect example of his work. Dimensionally the watch has a formidable case size measuring 50 mm × 20 mm (excluding the crown). They also made five smaller models with a 46 mm diameter. What makes this timepiece so special is the hand-sculpted solid bronze case with a porthole style sapphire crystal lens that intimately displays the time via two rotating discs. At the heart of the watch is a historical Fontainemelon 17-jewel manual winding movement dating to 1955. The timepiece is limited to ten pieces and originally retailed for $8,000.

Tourbillon of Tourbillons, 5. Switzerland

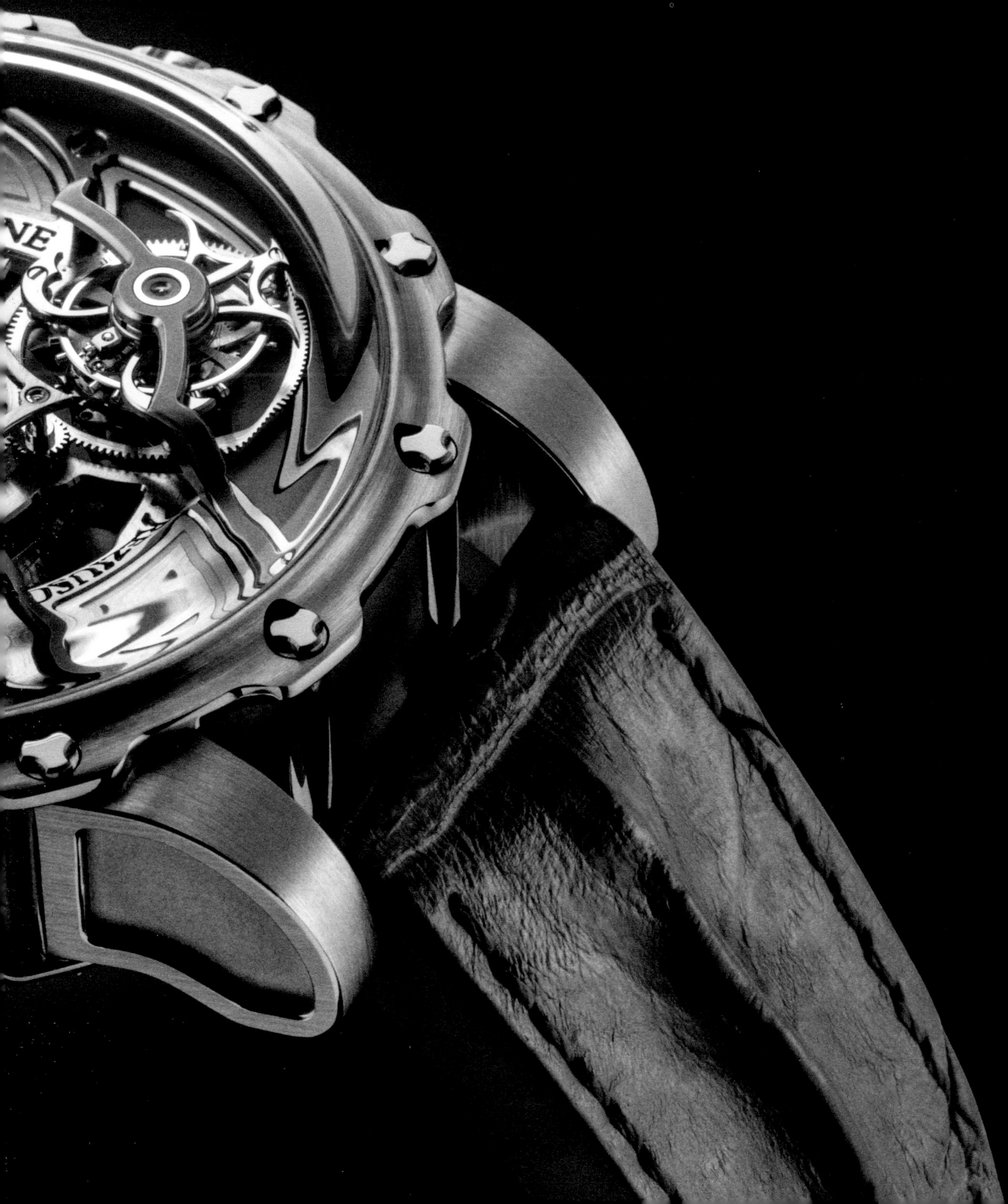

Tourbillon of Tourbillons, 5. Switzerland

Antoine Preziuso Tourbillon of Tourbillons

Antoine Preziuso is renowned in the watch industry for creating highly complicated luxurious timepieces. His new Tourbillon of Tourbillons is an exceptionally stylish watch that perfectly showcases his skills. The timepiece has a well-proportioned case measuring 45 mm × 14 mm that is constructed from 18-karat gold, titanium, and steel. What makes this watch so impressive is the wonderfully handcrafted multi-layered dial, which not only tells the time, but also displays three rotating planetary satellite tourbillons. Other details include a hand-engraved case and skeletonized hour/minute hands. Powering the watch is a patented 65-jewel mechanical hand-winding movement.

Tourbillon, 1. Switzerland

Antoine Tavan 1805 Bird Of Paradise Tourbillon

Antoine Tavan 1805 is a high-end watchmaker in Switzerland. The company is the brainchild of Roger Zarzosa, who has previously worked with brands like Christophe Claret, Zenith, Ulysse Nardin, and Manufacture La Joux Perret. Each of his watches are unique 1/1 pieces, including this sublime tourbillon. With a luxurious 18-karat rose gold case measuring 46 mm, the watch is designed for the discerning collector. What makes this timepiece so extraordinary is the sublime open-worked dial depicting a bird of paradise composed of 135 diamonds. Beneath the opulent façade is a sophisticated 19-jewel tourbillon movement that has a power reserve of 100 hours.

Minotaur, 5. Finland

Antti Rönkkö Minotaur

Antti Rönkkö is a small boutique watchmaker in Espoo, Finland. Following the success of his wonderful Steel Labyrinth, he has just unveiled another timepiece called the Minotaur. Dimensionally the watch displays modest proportions and has a black DLC (diamond-like carbon) treated stainless steel case measuring 42 mm × 11.75 mm. What makes this timepiece so special is the meticulous attention to detail. Other features include a hand-engraved multilayered dial with open-worked large Roman numerals and dual rotating full moon and dark moon indications. At the heart of the watch is a customized 25-jewel Swiss Soprod A10 mechanical self winding movement. The timepiece is limited to five pieces and is priced at $21,753.

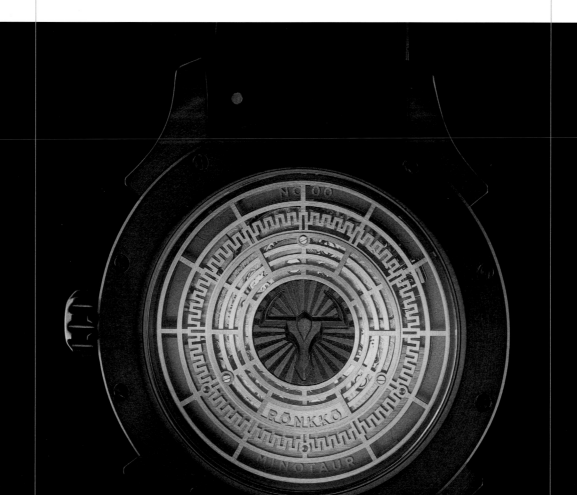

L09 Small Seconds (Titanium with Alligator Strap), 150. Switzerland

Armand Nicolet L09
Small Seconds

Armand Nicolet, who was the son of a watchmaker, originally established his own company in Tramelan, Switzerland, nearly 140 years ago. Primarily they are known for their innovative designs and high level of craftsmanship. The L09 Small Seconds is a striking watch that perfectly illustrates this point. Dimensionally the timepiece has a well-proportioned titanium case measuring 44 mm × 15 mm (excluding the crown). What makes this watch stand out is the stylish skeletonized dial. Other features include a rotating titanium bezel, small second sub counter (located at six o'clock), and anti-reflective sapphire crystal on both sides. Beneath the elegant exterior lies a vintage mechanical manual winding movement dating to 1957. The timepiece is limited to 150 pieces and is priced at $7,510.

Tourbillon Gumball 3000, 5. Germany

Armin Strom Tourbillon Gumball 3000

Armin Strom is a specialist watchmaker in the picturesque town of Burgdorf, located northwest of Bern in Switzerland. The brand is generally known for its exceptional level of craftsmanship and meticulous attention to detail. One of their newest models, the Tourbillon Gumball 3000, perfectly illustrates this point. This watch has a well-proportioned 18-karat rose gold case measuring 43.40 mm × 13.00 mm. What makes this timepiece so beautiful is the marvelous hand-decorated skeletonized dial. Other features include an offset black chapter ring with contrasting gold numerals and a large exposed tourbillon carriage (at nine o'clock). At the heart of the watch is a 24-jewel mechanical hand-winding movement designed in house.

Arnold & Son Time Pyramid Guilloché

Arnold & Son is a Swiss-owned company that draws inspiration from legendary watchmakers John and Roger Arnold; presently La Joux-Perret SA owns the business. The Time Pyramid Guilloché is one of their more distinctive models and pays homage to a British skeleton clock produced around 1830–1845. With an 18-karat gold case measuring 44.6 mm, this watch is designed to make a bold first impression. What makes this timepiece so elegant is the marvellous hand-decorated gold skeletonized Guilloché dial. Other features include an open-worked sub dial (at six o'clock) displaying hours/minutes and two power reserve indications. At the heart of the watch is a sophisticated 27-jewel twin barrel mechanical manual winding movement.

"Wheels Of Time," 28. Switzerland

AOS Watches
"Wheels Of Time"

Roland Stampfli established AOS Watches in 2010, in honor of his father, Arthur Oskar Stampfli. Within the last five years, the company has produced many interesting watches, including the phenomenal "Wheels of Time." This watch has a really unique tubular case design measuring 68 mm × 26.80 mm. The timepiece only weighs around 81 grams because it is constructed from aluminum. What makes this watch so stylish is the way the time is presented: hours and minutes are displayed by two rotating cylinders. Powering the watch is an in-house-designed and -developed flat motor mechanical movement. The timepiece is limited to only twenty-eight pieces and prices range from $46,251–$99,731.

chgraving for Artya

1/1 Swiss Made

ArtyA

Arabesque Tourbillon, 1, Switzerland

ArtyA Arabesque Tourbillon

ArtyA is an eclectic Swiss brand established in 2007 by former CEO of RJ Romain Jerome Yvan Arpa. Ultimately they are renowned for their outrageous designs and bold approach to watchmaking. The Arabesque Tourbillon is one of their latest unique 1/1 timepieces. The watch has a sizable case measuring 52.5 mm × 40 mm × 14.4 mm. What makes this timepiece so outstanding is its hand-engraved titanium case with solid 24-karat gold inlays. Other features include an exquisite Arabesque dial, carbon bridges, and a large aperture displaying the sublime flying tourbillon. Beneath the luxurious façade lies a manual winding mechanical movement with a power reserve of 72 hours. The price of this timepiece is $227,451.

Grand Tourbillon Repetition Minute TB-RM1, 10. Switzerland

Ateliers deMonaco Grand Tourbillon Repetition Minute TB-RM1

Ateliers deMonaco is a small independent watchmaker situated in one of the world's most sought-after locations, Monaco. The Grand Tourbillon Repetition Minute TB-RM1 is one of their more exclusive models and was unveiled at Baselworld in 2010. With a rectangular case constructed of 55 individual parts and measuring 50 mm × 46 mm × 16 mm, this timepiece is designed to make a bold statement. What makes this watch so seductive is the beautiful skeletonized dial with hand-cut Roman numerals. Other features include open-worked hour/minute hands and a large patented one-minute tourbillon. Powering the timepiece is a bespoke mechanical movement oscillating at a frequency of 28,800 vibrations per hour.

2015 Royal Oak Laptimer Chronograph, 221. Switzerland

Audemars Piguet Royal Oak Laptimer Chronograph

Audemars Piguet is renowned for its beautifully designed Royal Oak range of watches. One of the latest creations is the sublime Royal Oak Laptimer Chronograph; this amazing timepiece is a tribute to the legendary Formula 1 driver Michael Schumacher. With a forged carbon and titanium case measuring 44 mm, this watch promises to be extra lightweight. What makes this timepiece so cool is the minimalistic skeletonized sporty dial. Other details include a black ceramic bezel, 18-karat screw-down crown, and stylized open-worked hour/minute hands. Beneath the robust exterior lies a sophisticated 34-jewel mechanical self-winding movement.

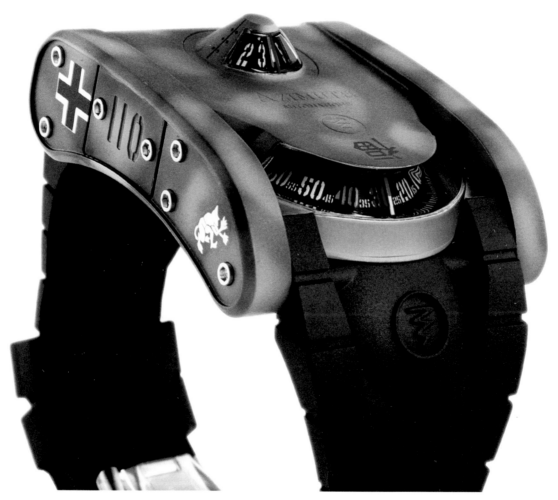

SP-1 Landship Battletank, 25. Singapore

Azimuth SP-1 Landship Battletank Collection

Azimuth is an exciting contemporary watchmaker based in the heart of Singapore. All of their timepieces perfectly combine humor and style. The Battletank collection are customized versions of their highly popular SP-1 Landship. With lightweight cases measuring 51 mm × 44 mm × 20 mm, these watches are designed to get noticed. A professional local artist has meticulously painted each individual case to appear like a miniature historic army tank, meaning each timepiece is completely unique and highly exclusive. At the heart of the watch is a customized ETA 2824-2 25-jewel mechanical self-winding movement.

R50, 10. France

B.R.M. R50

B.R.M. is an avant-garde watchmaker owned and operated by Bernard Richards. The company manufactures all their watches in France and is renowned for their meticulous attention to detail. The R50 is one of their most striking and distinctive watches to date. The watch has a massive titanium case measuring 50 mm × 16 mm (excluding the crown). What makes this timepiece so incredible is the minimalistic skeletonized dial. Other features include lightweight drilled vibrant-red hour/minute hands and a large rotating tourbillon (at nine o'clock). Powering the watch is an exclusive Swiss-made mechanical self-winding movement.

Elegance Chronographe, 41. Switzerland

Basse Broye Elegance Chronographe

Basse Broye is a small independent watchmaker in the heart of Switzerland. Entrepreneur Andreas Knecht and watchmaker Lénaïc Tschanz established the brand in 2014. The Elegance Chronographe is probably their most complicated and stylish model to date. With a stainless steel case diameter measuring 43.6 mm, the watch is designed to make a subtle statement. What makes this watch so eye catching is the intricate skeletonized black dial with contrasting silver Roman numerals. Other charming features include two sporty black sub dials, intricate hour/minute hands, and a sapphire crystal lens. At the heart of the watch is a mechanical self-winding 25-jewel Swiss-made Valjoux 7750 movement. This timepiece is limited to forty-one pieces.

Minuteur Tourbillon, 30. France

Bell & Ross Minuteur Tourbillon

Bell & Ross is an independent luxury watchmaker in Paris, France. All of their timepieces are distinctive in appearance and designed for professionals. The Minuteur Tourbillon is their most exclusive model and is limited to only thirty pieces. This watch is probably their largest model to date, with a lightweight titanium case measuring 50 mm × 44 mm. What makes this timepiece so interesting is the slick carbon fiber dial with contrasting white numerals. Other features include a small seconds sub dial, titanium/rubber dial, and a large aperture (at five o'clock) displaying the majestic tourbillon. Beneath the robust exterior lies a bespoke Swiss-made mechanical hand-winding movement.

Full Skeleton Floral, 1. Germany

Benzinger Full Skeleton Floral

Benzinger is a small boutique German brand that specializes in producing unique 1/1 custom-made watches. The company is solely owned and operated by master watchmaker Jochen Benzinger. One of his latest creations is the marvelous Full Skeleton Floral. Dimensionally the watch exudes traditional proportions and has a 42 mm diameter case; what makes this watch so astounding is the amazing level of detail. The skeletonized gold decorated floral dial is a work of art and displays an enormous level of craftsmanship. At the heart of the watch is a 17-jewel mechanical Swiss-made Unitas 6498 manual winding movement.

Primus, 9. Hungary

Bexei Watches Primus

Bexei Watches is a luxury watch manufacturer in Budapest, Hungary; the company is owned and operated by third generation watchmaker Aaron Becsei. All his timepieces are produced in exceptionally limited numbers, including the phenomenal Primus. With an opulent 18-karat gold case measuring 46 mm × 38 mm × 17.9 mm, the watch is designed for the discerning collector. What makes this timepiece so stunning is the exquisite hand-engraved silver dial. Other features include three gold sub dials and a large aperture (at nine o'clock) displaying the formidable tri-axial tourbillon carriage. Beneath the sublime exterior lies a highly complicated hand-crafted mechanical manual winding movement.

IP3.0, 24. Germany

BONHOFF UG IP3.0

BONHOFF is a new contemporary watch brand in the heart of Berlin, Germany. The company is the brainchild of designer and engineer Dr. Hannes Bonhoff. So far they have only released one exciting model called the UG IP3.0. Dimensionally the watch has a well-proportioned case measuring 44.3 mm × 13.9 mm. What makes this timepiece so special is the unconventional way time is presented: hours/minutes are displayed on demand (via small round windows) by turning the bezel, giving the watch a unique futuristic appearance. Other features include a patented hand-stitched integrated black leather strap. At the heart of the watch is a customized Swiss-made 25-jewel self-winding mechanical ETA 2824-2 movement.

Marie-Antoinette N°1160, 1. Switzerland

Breguet Marie-Antoinette
N°1160

In the world of horology, the name Breguet is synonymous with fine watchmaking. Although Abraham-Louis Breguet established the original business in 1775, it is now owned and operated by the Swatch Group. The Marie-Antoinette N°1160 is the company's most ambitious creation to date and is considered by many to be the fifth-most complicated watch in the world. Dimensionally the pocket watch has a huge yellow gold case measuring 63 mm × 26.2 mm. What makes this timepiece so incredible is the exceptionally detailed hand-decorated skeletonized dial. At the heart of the watch is a highly accomplished Swiss-made 63-jewel self-winding mechanical movement.

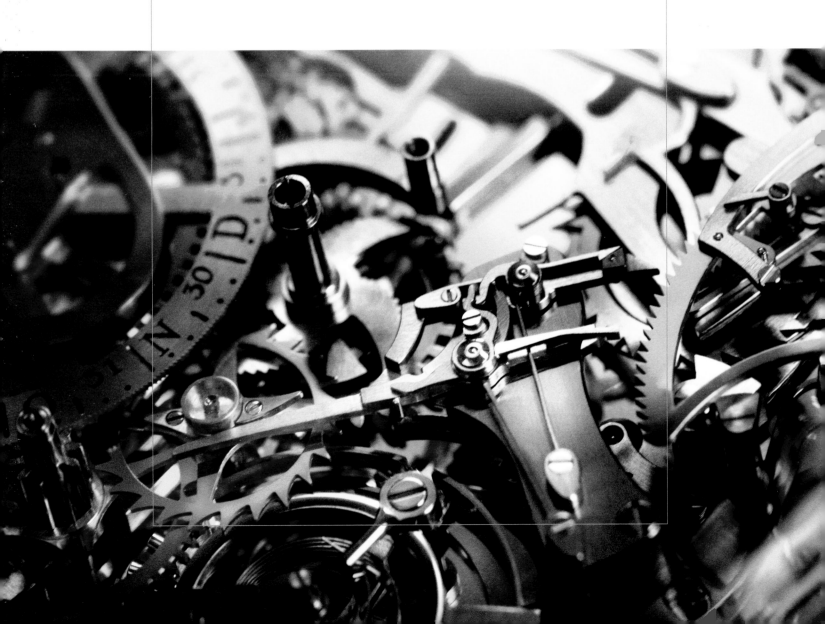

Wright Flyer White Gold, 50. England

Bremont Wright Flyer-White Gold

Bremont is a high quality British watchmaker situated in picturesque Henley-on-Thames. Aircraft enthusiasts Nick and Giles English established the company in 2002. One of their latest and most exciting offerings is the supreme Wright Flyer. This watch has an elegant 18-karat white gold case measuring 43mm x 14mm. What makes this timepiece so appealing is the specially designed rotor containing original muslin material that used to cover the 1903 Wright Flyer aircraft. Other features include an understated white dial with contrasting gold numbers and small seconds sub dial (at 9 o'clock). Powering the watch is an exclusive 25-jewel Swiss-made mechanical self-winding movement.

Génie 03, 55. Switzerland

Breva Génie 03

Swiss watch brand Breva derives its name from a warm southerly wind around Lake Como (northern Italy) called La Breva. The youthful and entrepreneurial Vincent Dupontreué established the company in 2013. His latest Génie 03 watch was recently unveiled at the 2015 Baselworld watch fair. This timepiece is slightly smaller than previous models and has a titanium case measuring 44.70 mm × 15.70 mm. What makes the watch so unique is a built-in functional anemometer that can measure wind speeds. Other features include a brilliant multi-layered dial, blue sub dial, and a twin-crown operating system. Beneath the durable exterior is an in-house 34-jewel mechanical self-winding movement.

One Tourbillon, 25. Switzerland

Buben & Zorweg One Tourbillon

Buben & Zorweg is a luxury goods brand based in Gröbming, Austria. In addition to safes and various storage solutions they also manufacture watches. The One Tourbillon is an exclusive watch limited to only twenty-five pieces worldwide. Its generous 18-karat rose gold case measures 48 mm. What makes this watch so elegant is the understated open-worked white dial with contrasting gold numerals. Other exquisite details include skeletonized gold hour/minute hands and a large aperture (at six o'clock) displaying the large rotating tourbillon carriage. At the heart of the watch is a 49-jewel manufactured hand-winding mechanical movement.

Experiment ZR012, 12. Switzerland

C3H5N3O9 Experiment ZR012

C3H5N3O9 is not a luxury brand, but more of an experimental platform. The project combines the talents of Urwerk and MB & F (Maximilian Büsser & Friends). So far they have only produced one timepiece, called the Experiment ZR012. This watch is constructed from lightweight zirconium and has a massive case measuring 55 mm × 44 mm. What makes this timepiece so extraordinary is the highly complicated multi-layered avant-garde dial: two Reuleaux polygon rotors tracing epitrochoid curves display hours and minutes. The revolutionary Wankel engine inspired the original concept of the watch. Beneath the futuristic façade lies an exclusive 42-jewel mechanical manual winding movement developed by Cyrano Devanthey.

Triple Axis Tourbillon, 135. Switzerland

Cabestan Triple Axis Tourbillon

Cabestan is one of the most innovative luxury watchmakers in the industry. Presently dynamic businessman Lionel Betoux owns the company. The Triple Axis is the company's fourth offering and was unveiled at Baselworld 2015. The watch exudes "XL" proportions and measures 50.25 mm × 45.50 mm × 22.30 mm. What makes this timepiece so impressive is the contemporary architectural 18-karat gold case with sapphire crystal windows. Another fantastic feature is its open-worked dial perfectly exposing the sensational three-dimensional tourbillon carriage. At the heart of the watch is an incredibly complicated Fusée-and-Chain-driven mechanical hand-winding movement containing 1,044 individual components.

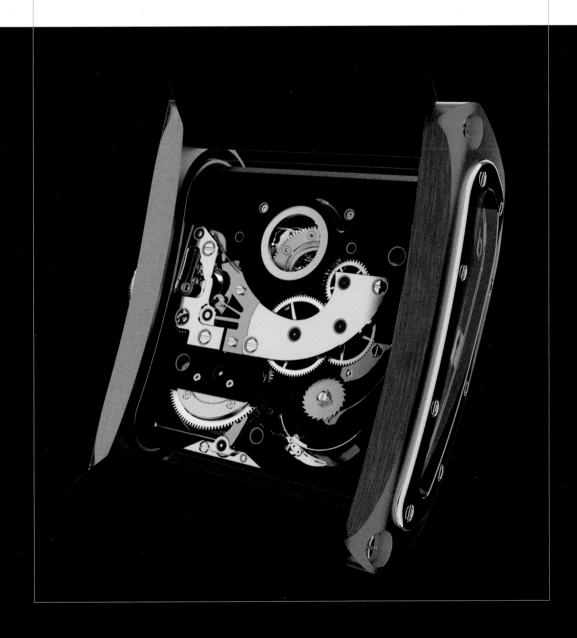

Patravi TravelTec 4X, 125. Switzerland

Carl F. Bucherer Patravi TravelTec 4X

Carl F. Bucherer is an independent brand based in the heart of Lucerne, Switzerland. The company was originally established in 1888, and for over 125 years has been at the forefront of fine watchmaking. A great example of their fine craftsmanship is the Patravi TravelTec 4X. The watch has a generously proportioned luxurious 18-karat rose gold case measuring 46.6 mm × 15.5 mm. What makes this model so striking is the exquisite multi-layered skeletonized dial that delicately exposes various mechanical elements of the watch. Other features include a black ceramic dial, sporty chronograph sub counters, and a triple time zone indication. Powering the watch is a refined Swiss-made 39-jewel automatic movement.

Rotonde de Cartier Astrotourbillon
Skeleton Watch, 100. France

Cartier Rotonde de Cartier Astrotourbillon Skeleton Watch

French jewelery and watch manufacturer Cartier epitomizes class and sophistication. The company was privately owned until 1964, and is now part of the Richemont Group. One of their most exclusive creations is the wonderful Rotonde de Cartier Astrotourbillon Skeleton Watch. This timepiece displays generous proportions and has a luxurious 18-karat gold case measuring 47 mm × 15.8 mm. What makes this watch so special is the sublime minimalistic multi-layered dial. Other exquisite details include three-dimensional Roman numerals, understated blue hour/minute hands, and a marvelous flying tourbillon (at ten o'clock). Beneath the refined exterior lies a bespoke 23-jewel Swiss-made mechanical hand-winding movement.

L.U.C Engine One H, 100. Switzerland

Chopard L.U.C Engine One H

Chopard is a luxury watchmaker situated in the heart of Geneva, Switzerland. The company was originally established in 1860 by Louis-Ulysse Chopard and is still privately owned today. One of their more exclusive timepieces is the phenomenal L.U.C. Engine One H, which has a well-proportioned lightweight titanium case measuring 44.50 mm × 35 mm × 10.35 mm. What makes this timepiece so attractive is the automotive-inspired three-dimensional open-worked dial, giving the watch a refined and sporty appearance. Functionally the timepiece features hours, minutes, small seconds, tourbillon, and power reserve indication. At the heart of the watch is a 29-jewel mechanical hand-winding movement composed of 232 parts.

X-TREM-1, 8. Switzerland

Christophe Claret X-TREM-1

Christophe Claret is recognized by his contemporaries as a watchmaker of distinction. Prior to establishing his own company, he developed many extremely complex movements for other Swiss watch brands. The X-TREM 1 is one of their finest and most exclusive timepieces to date. An oversized case measures 40.80 mm × 56.80 mm × 15 mm. What makes this timepiece so amazing is the way the time is presented: magnetically driven spheres in two cylindrical tubes magically display hours and minutes. Other distinctive features include a skeletonized dial with numeral indications and a large exposed tourbillon carriage (at six o'clock). Powering the watch is a refined 64-jewel twin barrel mechanical hand-winding movement. Priced at $308,000.

Wristmaster, 100. Germany

Chronoswiss Wristmaster

Chronoswiss is widely regarded in the world of horology as a high-class watch manufacturer. Gerd R. Lang established the company in 1983 in Munich, Germany, and later relocated their headquarters to Lucerne, Switzerland. The Wristmaster was inspired by a time-keeping instrument called the Bordmaster, which was originally installed in the dashboard of vintage cars. This model is one of the world's largest watches, with a mammoth case measuring 84 mm × 42.20 mm. What makes this timepiece so unique is its bold and distinctive industrial appearance. Functionally the watch has two dials featuring hours, minutes, seconds, and a separate chronograph timer. Beneath the formidable exterior are two individual Swiss-made mechanical self-winding movements.

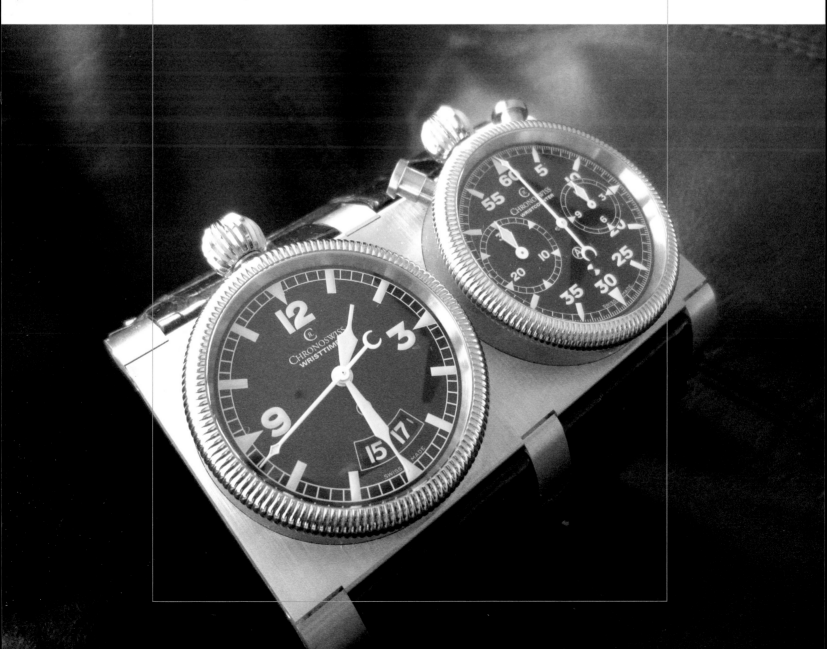

Hydroscaph H140 Carbon, 140. Switzerland

Clerc Hydroscaph H140 Carbon

Clerc is a small boutique watchmaker in the heart of Geneva, Switzerland. Although they have a history dating back to 1874, Gerald Clerc currently operates and manages the business. Recently the company celebrated their 140th anniversary, and to commemorate the event they unveiled the Hydroscaph H140 Carbon. The watch is well proportioned, with a diameter measuring 44 mm (49.6 mm including lateral protectors). What makes this timepiece so attractive is the super-lightweight angular forged carbon case. Other features include a matte black dial with contrasting white numerals and sporty sub counters. At the heart of the watch is a 51-jewel Swiss-made mechanical self-winding chronograph movement.

Corum Admiral's Cup Legend 42 60th Anniversary Tourbillon, 60. Switzerland

Corum Admiral's Cup Legend 42 60th Anniversary Tourbillon

Corum is a luxury watchmaker in the picturesque La Chaux De Fonds, Switzerland. This year, the company celebrated its 60th anniversary and released a watch called the Admiral's Cup Legend 42 60th Anniversary Tourbillon to mark the occasion. The timepiece displays modest proportions and has an 18-karat gold case measuring 42 mm × 13 mm. What makes this watch so impressive is the distinctive twelve-sided bezel and transparent brown dial. Other features include a retrograde date indication, open-worked gold hour/minute hands, and a large aperture (at six o'clock) displaying the flying tourbillon. Powering the watch is a Swiss-made manual winding tourbillon movement with a power reserve of seventy-two hours.

20'000 FEET Carbon Dial,
250. Switzerland

CX Swiss Military 20,000 Feet Carbon Fiber Dial

CX Swiss Military was first established over fifty years ago in Bubendorf/Switzerland; the business is now owned and operated by the dynamic Frank M. Bürgin. Although all of their models are attractive, they are ultimately known for their formidable 20,000 Feet. The watch has a massive titanium case measuring 46 mm × 30 mm. What makes this timepiece so unique is the fact it holds the world record in the category of automatic diving watches. Other features include a black carbon fiber dial with large luminous indexes and red accented sub counters. At the heart of the watch is a Swiss-made Valjoux ETA 7750 25-jewel self-winding chronograph movement.

Dream Watch DW5, made to order. Switzerland

De Bethune
Dream Watch 5

Within thirteen years De Bethune has established themselves as one of the most innovative watchmakers in the world of horology. Presently David Zanetta, Denis Flageollet, and Pierre Jacques own the business. The Dream Watch 5 epitomizes the company's creativity and attention to detail. This watch is exceptionally well proportioned and measures 49 mm × 39 mm × 11 mm. What makes this timepiece so striking is the perfectly sculpted polished titanium case. This characteristic gives the watch a unique futuristic appearance. Functionally the watch displays jumping hours, analogue minutes (via a rotating disc), and a three dimensional spherical moon phase indication. Powering the watch is a sophisticated 32-jewel twin barrel movement composed of 329 individual parts.

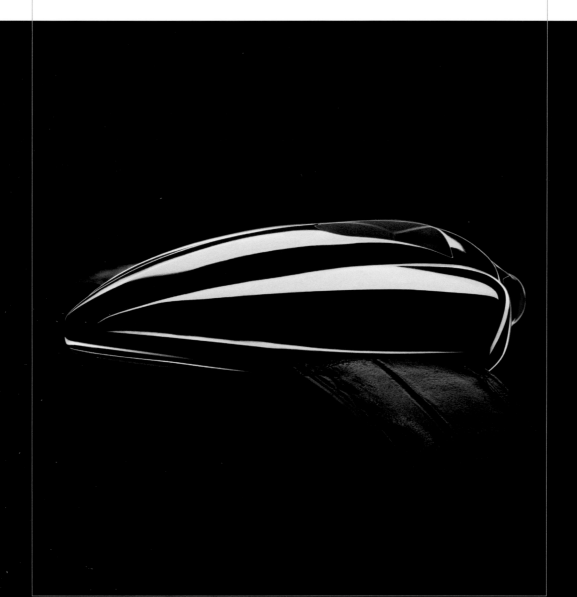

Star Wars, 500. USA

Devon Star Wars

Devon is an innovative watchmaker based in the vibrant city of Los Angeles, California. Progressive designer and conceptual artist Scott Devon established the company in 2010. One of their latest creations is a collaboration with legendary George Lucas, appropriately called Star Wars. With a black DLC (diamond-like carbon) stainless steel case measuring 53.3 mm × 19 mm, the watch exudes muscular proportions. What makes this timepiece so amazing is the meticulous attention to detail. The composition ingeniously incorporates elements from Darth Vader's helmet and the formidable TIE Fighter (the starship of the Imperial fleet). Beneath the robust exterior lies a complicated (patented) electromechanical belt-driven system.

Twenty-8-Eight Skeleton Tourbillon
Titanium, 5. Switzerland

Dewitt Twenty-8-Eight
Skeleton Tourbillon Titanium

Dewitt is a Swiss company at the forefront of haute horlogerie. A direct descendant of Emperor Napoléon called Jérôme de Witt founded the business. Within twelve years he has designed many exciting watches, including the Twenty-8-Eight Skeleton Tourbillon Titanium. Dimensionally the timepiece displays modest proportions and has a case diameter of 43 mm. What makes this watch so appealing is the incredible three-dimensional blue skeletonized dial that gives the watch a dynamic architectural appearance. Other features include a distinctive hour/minute hand and a large rotating tourbillon (at six o'clock). Beneath the elegant façade lies a Swiss-made 19-jewel mechanical hand-winding movement.

Type 46, 1. Canada

Division Furtive Type 46

Division Furtive is a small independent watchmaker located in Montréal, Canada; microelectronic engineer Gabriel Ménard launched the company after he was made redundant at his previous employer. The Type 46 is definitely his most exclusive (one piece) and complicated timepiece to date. With a sterling silver case measuring 50 mm × 16 mm, the watch is designed to make a bold statement. What makes it so special is the amazing futuristic matte black dial. Time is displayed in a linear format via two three-dimensional gold cursers. Functionally the timepiece features hours, minutes, triple time zones, and moon phase indication. At the heart of the watch is a state-of-the-art Swiss-made electromechanical stepper motor.

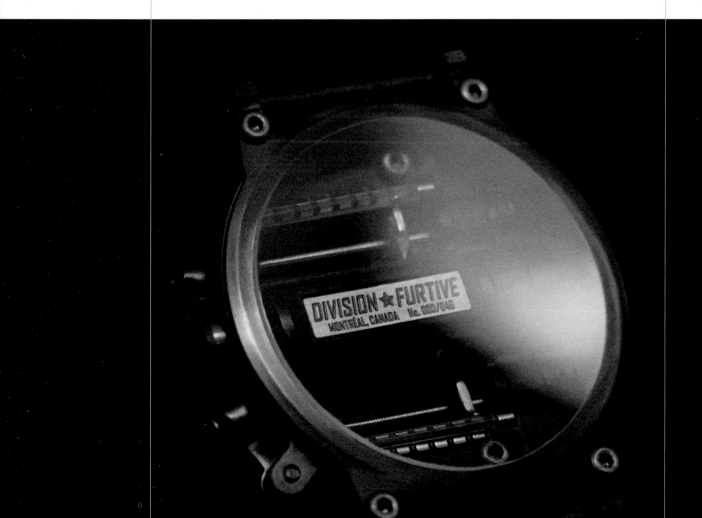

Coeur Blanc, 1. Switzerland

Dubey & Schaldenbrand SA
Coeur Blanc

Dubey & Schaldenbrand SA is a high-quality watchmaker situated in idyllic La Chaux-de-Fonds, Switzerland. Although the company was established in 1946, the youthful and dynamic Jonatan Gil now manages the business. The Coeur Blanc is probably the most luxurious and exclusive (one piece) timepiece they have produced to date. With a sensational 18-karat white gold case measuring 45 mm, this creation will definitely appeal to watch aficionados. What makes this watch so amazing is the wonderful gem set case, bezel, and open heart dial. The timepiece is garnished with 709 sparkling diamond baguettes (22.55 carats). Beneath the opulent exterior lies a highly complicated 18-jewel Swiss-made hand-winding mechanical tourbillon movement.

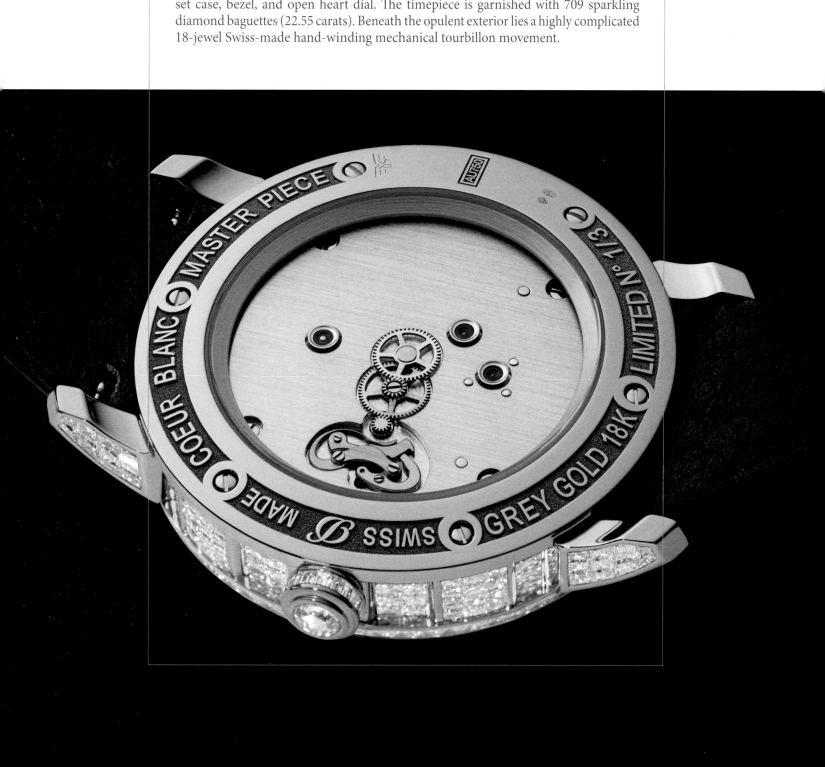

Tourbillon, 5. Switzerland

Emile Chouriet Tourbillon

Emile Chouriet was a legendary seventeenth century Geneva-based watchmaker; in 1997, Jean Depéry established a luxury brand of the same name. For nearly two decades the company has been producing a range of exquisite timepieces. Probably the most opulent creation to date is the supreme Tourbillon. This timepiece exudes classical proportions and has a luxurious 18-karat gold case measuring 40 mm. What makes this watch superlative is the beautiful open-worked solid gold dial; this marvelous characteristic perfectly exposes various mechanical elements of the watch. Other features include intricate gold hour/minute hands and a large rotating tourbillon (at six o'clock). Powering the timepiece is a bespoke manual winding movement with Cotes de Genève decoration.

Complication One Platinum, 16. Switzerland

Emmanuel Bouchet
Complication One Platinum

Master watchmaker Emmanuel Bouchet is based in the heart of London, England. Born into a family of jewelers, he established his own luxury brand in 2014. The Complication One is his first timepiece and is available in a variety of different materials; the most extravagant is the sensational 44 mm × 11.20 mm platinum version. What makes this watch so exceptional is the distinctive multi-layered three-dimensional black dial that perfectly exposes the escape wheel and anchor. Other features include three sapphire discs (displaying hours, minutes, and seconds) and polished sapphire tip hands. Beneath the refined façade lies a Swiss-made twin barrel manual movement composed of 283 individual components.

Ari Watch, 2. Australia

Eva Leube Ari Watch

Eva Leube is a small independent watchmaker in vibrant Sydney, Australia. After working for companies like Ulysse Nardin and Thomas Prescher she finally established her own brand in 2007. The Ari Watch is her first exciting creation and is named after her first-born child. Dimensionally the timepiece has very unusual proportions and measures 52.44 mm × 21.6 mm × 8.45 mm. What makes this watch so captivating is the incredible curved case with three sapphire crystal windows. Other features include a magnificent open-worked dial (exposing various mechanical elements of the watch) and a top-mounted crown. Powering the watch is a Swiss-made 18-jewel hand-winding movement containing 209 components.

Celebration Skull, 24. Switzerland

Fiona Krüger Skull

Even though Fiona Krüger was born in Scotland, she now resides in La Chaux de Fonds. After she attained a masters of advanced studies in design she began creating her own watches. The Skull is her first unique timepiece and all its components were manufactured in Switzerland. With a stainless steel case measuring 57.4 mm × 41.3 mm × 10.3 mm, the watch is designed to make a bold first impression. What makes this timepiece so striking is the bespoke skull-shaped skeletonized dial with hand-painted gold lacquer décor, giving the watch a cool gothic appearance. Other features include an ornate crown and delicate blue galvanized brass hour/minute hands. At the heart of the watch is a 34-jewel twin barrel hand-winding movement sourced from Technotime.

10 Years Anniversary Tourbillon, 10. Switzerland

FP Journe Tourbillon Souverain

FP Journe is a specialist luxury watch brand situated in the heart of Geneva, Switzerland. Master craftsman François-Paul Journe established the company in 1999. One of his most striking creations is his award-winning (Grand Prix d'Horlogerie de Genève 2004) Tourbillon Souverain. The watch exudes modest proportions and has an opulent 40 mm 18-karat gold case. What makes this timepiece so extraordinary is the exquisite multi-layered façade. Other sublime features include a silver Guilloché dial with a small second counter and large aperture (at nine o'clock) displaying the rotating tourbillon carriage. Powering the watch is a sophisticated 26-jewel rose gold mechanical hand-winding movement.

Inaccessible Tourbillon Minute Repeater,
1. Switzerland

Franc Vila Inaccessible Tourbillon Minute Repeater FVn N°3

Franc Vila is renowned in the world of horology for producing high-quality and distinctive watches. Passionate Spanish designer Franc Vila created the brand in 2004. The Inaccessible Tourbillon Minute Repeater was unveiled at Baselworld 2015 and is their most ambitious timepiece to date. With an enormous 18-karat red gold case measuring 52 mm × 48 mm × 15.3 mm, the watch definitely asserts authority. What makes this watch so appealing is the meticulously hand-crafted skeletonized dial. Other features include distinctive triangular indexes, diamond-shape hands, and a large exposed flying tourbillon (at six o'clock). Beneath the luxurious façade lies a Swiss-made mechanical hand-winding movement with a ninety-hour power reserve.

Aeternitas-mega-4, 1. Switzerland

Franck Muller
Aeternitas-mega-4

Franck Muller is a high-end watch brand in the picturesque village of Genthod (close to Geneva) in Switzerland. Passionate watchmakers Franck Muller and Vartan Sirmakes originally founded the business in 1991. Although they have created many exclusive watches, the formidable Aeternitas-mega-4 is definitely their magnum opus. In fact, it is probably the world's most complicated mechanical timepiece. What makes it so incredible is the astonishingly detailed hand-crafted silver dial. Functionally the watch has an impressive array of features, including dual time zones, perpetual calendar, and astronomic moon indication. At the heart of the watch is a sophisticated 99-jewel movement consisting of a staggering 1,483 individual components.

61 Planum Australe, 1. USA

Frank Heydrich 61
Planum Australe

Frank Heydrich is an independent watchmaker in Phoenix, Arizona. Effectively he manufactures watches in his spare time as he is a full-time jet engineer by trade. Each of his timepieces are made to order and every creation is totally unique. The Planum Australe is a brilliant example of his work and is the sixty-first watch he has ever created. What makes this timepiece so amazing is the handcrafted dial constructed from Mars meteorite; this material was discovered in Morocco and has a wonderful grainy texture. Other features include a brushed steel bezel and Silver Dauphine hour/minute hands (with white lume). Beneath the 42 mm stainless steel case is a 25-jewel Swiss-made Omega 2500C co-axial automatic mechanical movement.

Helios Titanium, 88. Switzerland

Frederic Jouvenot Helios
White Gold

Frederic Jouvenot is a small brand specializing in the production of haute horlogerie timepieces. The company is owned by Frederic Jouvenot and is in La Chaux-de-Fonds, Switzerland. One of their most distinctive and exclusive watches is the Helios White Gold. With a case measuring 44 mm × 55 mm × 13 mm, the timepiece is designed to make a bold statement. What makes this watch stand out from the crowd is the exquisite multi-layered white dial: minutes are displayed via a rotating central disc and jumping hours are illustrated by twelve sunbeams. Powering the watch is a hand-decorated Swiss-made 45-jewel mechanical manual winding movement.

Nixie One Watch, 50. Switzerland

Gelfman Design Nixie One Watch

Gelfman is a small Swiss-based company that manufactures a range of specialist microelectronic products. Progressive designer Ilya Gelfman is the creative force behind the brand. The Nixie One Watch is their first foray into the world of horology. A substantial 316L stainless steel case measures 59 mm × 40 mm × 20 mm. What makes this watch so unique is the perfectly sculpted futuristic façade; time is displayed via two Nixie tubes that flash intermittently on demand. Unlike most of the other mechanical watches featured in this book, this watch is powered by a rechargeable Li-ion battery, so the timepiece can be recharged on a regular basis and very quickly (80% in two hours).

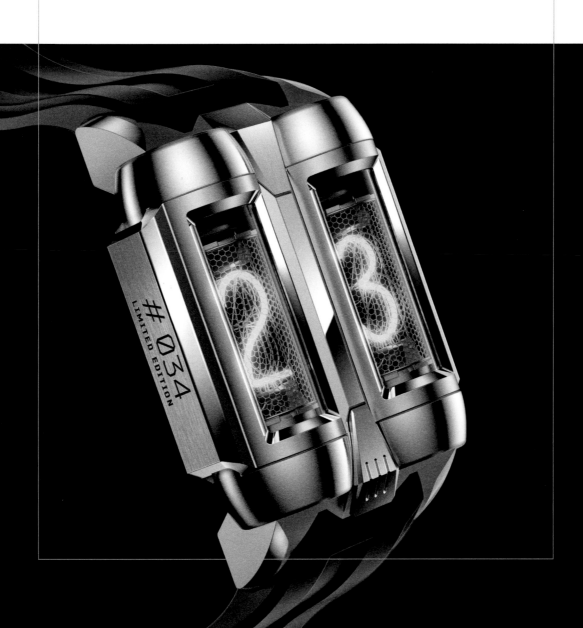

Tri-Axial Tourbillon, 20. Switzerland

Girard Perregaux Tri-Axial Tourbillon

The name Girard Perregaux is synonymous with the production of high quality watches. All of their exquisite timepieces are manufactured in La Chaux-de-Fonds, Switzerland. At Baselworld 2015 they unveiled a new interpretation of the already successful Tri-Axial Tourbillon. With an 18-karat white gold case measuring 48 mm × 16.83 mm (excluding the crown), this is one of the company's largest watches to date. What makes this timepiece so special is the striking three-dimensional architectural grill style dial. Features like a rotating tourbillon encased in dome sapphire crystal and retrograde power reserve are cohesive. Beneath the luxurious façade lies an intricate 34-jewel Swiss-made hand-wound mechanical movement.

PanoInverse White Gold, 200. Germany

Glashütte Original
PanoInverse

Glashütte Original is a German watchmaker well known for their meticulous attention to detail. The company has a heritage dating back over 165 years and was originally established by Ferdinand Adolph Lange. Even though the PanoInverse was released in 2008, it is still one of their most distinctive models. It exudes modest proportions and has a stainless steel case measuring 42 mm × 12 mm. What makes this timepiece so eye-catching is its black galvanized open-worked dial with complimentary white gold hour/minute hands. At the heart of the watch is an accomplished hand-decorated/finished 31-jewel mechanical manual winding movement with a power reserve of forty-one hours.

Geo Graham Tourbillon Orrery, 20. Switzerland

Graham SA Geo Graham Tourbillon Orrery

Graham SA is a high-end watchmaker situated in picturesque La Chaux-de-Fonds, Switzerland. The company is privately owned and inspired by the works of the legendary eighteenth century English inventor George Graham. Recently they unveiled their most exclusive and complicated timepiece to date, called the Geo Graham Tourbillon Orrery. With a luxurious 18-karat pink gold case measuring 48 mm × 17.60 mm, the watch is designed to be noticed. What makes this timepiece so exceptional is the wonderful black open-worked dial with hand-engraved exposed central Tourbillon. Other features include a Gregorian calendar, Zodiac scale, and three-dimensional solar indication. Powering the watch is a 35-jewel Swiss-made twin barrel hand-winding mechanical movement.

Diamond Set Tourbillon 24 Secondes Contemporain, 1. Switzerland

Greubel Forsey Diamond Set Tourbillon 24 Secondes Contemporain

Greubel Forsey is rapidly becoming one of the most prestigious watchmakers in the horology world. Robert Greubel and Stephen Forsey established the company in 2004. Although all of their timepieces are highly coveted, the Diamond Set Tourbillon 24 Secondes Contemporain is the most exclusive. The watch has a classical 18-karat white gold case measuring 43.5 mm × 16 mm. What makes this timepiece so astonishing is the sublime multi-layered cobalt blue gem set dial. Incredibly, the dial, lugs, and bezel are adorned with 272 flawless baguette diamonds. Other features include a retrograde power reserve indication and Paexposed tourbillon (at seven o'clock). Beneath the extravagant façade lies a 40-jewel Swiss-made twin barrel hand-winding mechanical movement.

Parallax Tourbillon, 5. Netherlands

Grönefeld Parallax Tourbillon

Grönefeld is a small independent luxury watchmaker in Oldenzaal, Netherlands. Dynamic brothers Tim and Bart Grönefeld founded the company in 2008. The Parallax Tourbillon is a great example of their work and was awarded the Grand Prix d'Horlogerie de Genève award in 2014 (best tourbillon). With an opulent platinum case measuring 43 mm × 12.5 mm, this watch will definitely attract the attention of serious collectors. What makes this timepiece so striking is the beautifully handcrafted solid sterling silver and gold-plated dial that works as a perfect backdrop for the blue hands and large exposed tourbillon. At the heart of the watch is a 27-jewel mechanical movement containing 278 individual components.

Midnight Sun, 5. Sweden

Gustafsson and Sjögren
Midnight Sun

GoS Watches (Gustafsson and Sjögren) is a small boutique brand situated in beautiful Linköping, Sweden. Craftsman Johan Gustafsson and watchmaker Patrik Sjögren established the company in 2007. The Midnight was unveiled in 2013 and showcases their meticulous attention to detail. Dimensionally the watch is well proportioned and has a diameter measuring 45 mm. What makes this timepiece so appealing is the distinctive hand-engraved Damascus steel case that works in perfect harmony with the 18-karat gold sunray pattern dial. Beneath the refined exterior lies a Swiss-made 17-jewel hand-winding mechanism customized and skeletonized by the extraordinarily talented Jochen Benzinger.

Venturer Tourbillon Dual Time Sapphire Skeleton, 1. Switzerland

H. Moser & Cie. Venturer Tourbillon Dual Time Sapphire Skeleton

H. Moser & Cie is a small independent family-owned watchmaking business; they pride themselves on manufacturing all of their timepieces at their own production facilities in Switzerland. The Venturer Tourbillon Dual Time Sapphire Skeleton was recently unveiled at Baselworld 2015. With a classical round case measuring 41.5 mm, the watch is designed to make a subtle statement. What makes this timepiece so unique is the handcrafted case made entirely from Sapphire crystal that perfectly showcases all the intricate mechanics of the skeletonized dial. At the heart of the watch is a refined self-winding movement with an 18-karat solid gold rotor.

Tourbillon Watch, 1. Japan

Hajime Asaoka
Tourbillon Watch

Hajime Asaoka is a contemporary watchmaker originating in Yokahama, Japan. Each of his timepieces is fastidiously made by hand in very limited numbers. Interestingly, he began his career as an industrial designer and then later taught himself the art of watchmaking. One of his most distinctive creations is the Tourbillon Watch, which was released in 2011 to a positive reception and displays modest proportions, with a diameter measuring 42 mm. What makes this watch so impressive is the bold graphite vertical patterned open-heart dial that perfectly showcases the large rotating tourbillon carriage. Powering the watch is an accomplished 17-jewel hand-winding mechanical movement.

H2 - Flying Resonance, 1. Switzerland

Haldimann H2 - Flying Resonance

Beat Haldimann is a small Swiss-based watchmaker who adheres to the finest traditional techniques. All of his timepieces are meticulously handcrafted and are calibrated to within a thousandth-millimeter. The H2 - Flying Resonance is not a current model, but does have a more conventional aesthetic than some of his later models. Dimensionally the watch is available in a 39 mm or 42 mm platinum case. What makes this timepiece so extraordinary is the striking three-dimensional white dial that perfectly exposes the intricate mechanics of the central double flying tourbillon. Other features include black Roman numerals and delicate hour/minute hands. Beneath the exquisite façade lies a refined triple barrel movement.

Histoire de Tourbillon 6, 20. Switzerland

Harry Winston Histoire de Tourbillon 6

Harry Winston is largely known for the production of high-class jewelry; recently they became part of the Swatch Group and are now going from strength to strength. The Histoire de Tourbillon 6 is one of their most exclusive watches and was presented at Baselworld 2015. With a luxurious 18-karat white gold contoured case measuring 55 mm × 49 mm, the timepiece is designed to make a striking statement. What makes this watch so awesome is its amazing futuristic appearance. Other details include a multi-layered dial with dual time zones and a separate window containing the tri-axial tourbillon. At the heart of the watch is a highly complicated Swiss-made mechanical movement containing 683 separate components.

Vortex, 88. Switzerland

Hautlence Vortex

Hautlence is an avant garde watchmaker based in the heart of Neuchâtel, Switzerland. The company is owned and operated by accomplished designer and CEO Guillaume Tetu. Recently they unveiled a new and exciting watch called the Vortex. It is one of the company's largest watches to date, measuring 52 mm × 50 mm × 17.8 mm. What makes the timepiece so outstanding is its architectural titanium case with numerous sapphire crystal windows giving the recipient a perfect view of its intricate mechanics from every angle. Time is cleverly displayed by retrograde minutes and jumping hours. Powering the watch is a 92-jewel Swiss-made self-winding movement containing 552 individual components.

No.16., 100. England

Hoptroff No.16

Hoptroff is an innovative watchmaker in London, England. British physicist Richard Hoptroff is the creative force behind the brand. Over the last few years he has developed many unique watches, including the formidable No.16. This amazing timepiece has a mammoth 18-karat gold case measuring 83.7 mm × 43.4 mm × 18.7 mm. What makes this watch so special is its dual art nouveau dials displaying a plethora of functions, including hours, minutes, equations of time, sunrise, sunset, and moon phase indications. It is also the world's most accurate timepiece and only loses 1½ seconds per thousand years. At the heart of the watch is a small atomic vessel (containing caesium) powered by a rechargeable battery.

MP-05 LAFERRARI BLACK, 50. Switzerland

Hublot MP-05 LAFERRARI Black

Hublot has become one of the world's largest brands, mostly due to the talents of Jean-Claude Biver, who invented their iconic Big Bang watches. The MP-05 LAFERRARI Black is one of the company's latest and most innovative watches. With a Microblasted Black (PVD treated) Titanium case measuring 45.8 mm × 39.5 mm × 15.30 mm, the watch is designed to be noticed. What makes this timepiece so incredible is the sensational futuristic open-worked dial showcasing its innovative in-house mechanism. Other features include cylindrical hour/minute indications and a large rotating tourbillon. Beneath the contemporary façade lies a complicated 108-jewel Swiss-made hand-winding movement that has a staggering fifty-day power reserve.

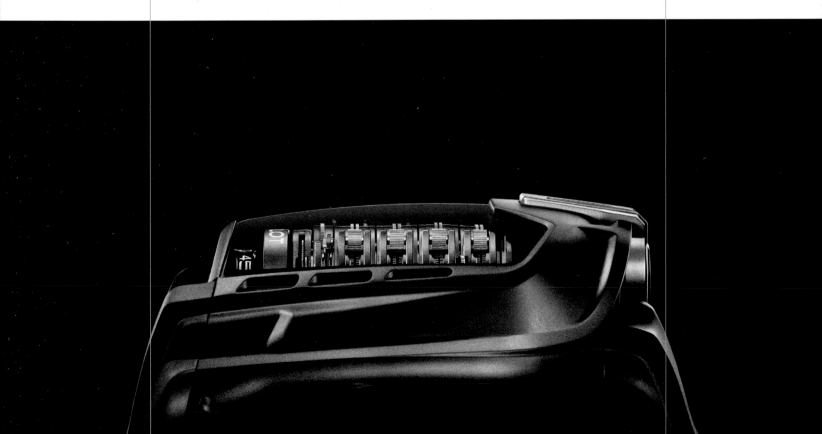

Abyss Tourbillon Four Elements-TETHYS, 30. Switzerland

Hysek SA Abyss Tourbillon Four Elements-TETHYS

Hysek SA is a contemporary watchmaker situated in the village of Lussy-sur-Morges in Switzerland. In 2000, Mr. Akram Aljord became the owner and CEO of the company. The Abyss Tourbillon Four Elements-TETHYS is one of their more exclusive timepieces and was originally unveiled in 2009. Dimensionally the watch exudes masculine proportions and has a case measuring 63 mm × 44 mm × 18 mm. What makes this watch really special is the stunning multi-layered skeletonized blue-tinted sapphire dial that exposes all the intricate mechanical parts of the watch. Other details include open-worked hour/minute hands and a diamond-set bezel. Powering the watch is an in-house 28-jewel automatic tourbillon movement comprising 338 individual parts.

H3, 25. Switzerland

HYT H3

HYT is an exceptionally creative luxury watchmaker in Neuchâtel, Switzerland and is the brainchild of charismatic and innovative designer Vincent Perriard. In 2015, they released their most exclusive and complicated watch to date, the H3. With a massive titanium and platinum case measuring 62 mm × 48.8 mm × 16 mm, the timepiece is designed to make a striking statement. What makes this watch so incredible is its complicated three-dimensional architectural dial, giving the timepiece a futuristic appearance. Other features include a fluid linear hour display and rotating retrograde minute indication. At the heart of the watch is a Swiss-made 53-jewel hand-winding movement with a 170-hour power reserve.

Zermatt V.II Limited Edition Mechanical Skeleton Watch, 6. USA

IceLink Zermatt V.II Limited Edition Mechanical Skeleton Watch

IceLink is a high-end jeweler and watch brand situated in glamorous Los Angeles, California. The company is family owned by Andy and Suzy Sogoyan. Of all their models, the 18K White Gold Zermatt V.II Limited Edition Mechanical Skeleton Watch is probably the most exclusive to date. The timepiece displays supersized proportions, measuring 67.3 mm × 42.6 mm. What makes this watch so extraordinary is its industrial-style open-worked black dial displaying six different time zones operated from one unique mechanism. Beneath the robust exterior lies an award-winning Swiss-made 43-jewel movement composed of 327 separate components.

Part Time DN.BL, 24. Israel

Itay Noy Part-Time

Itay Noy is a specialist independent award-winning watchmaker in Old Jaffa, Israel. Interestingly, as well as making superb timepieces he also teaches at Bezalel Academy of Arts and Design in Jerusalem. Recently at Baselworld he released a stylish watch appropriately called Part-Time. This timepiece features modest proportions and has a 316L stainless steel case measuring 41.6 mm × 44.6 mm, with a height of 10.6 mm. What makes this watch so distinctive is the frosty blue deconstructed textured façade, giving it a wonderful non-conventional and futuristic appearance. Functionally the watch displays hours, minutes, seconds, and sun/moon indications via several sub dials and windows. Powering the watch is a 17-jewel Swiss-made Unitas ETA 6498-1 mechanical hand-winding movement.

Ingenieur Constant-Force Tourbillon IW5900, 50. Switzerland

IWC Ingenieur Constant-Force Tourbillon IW5900

IWC (Independent Watch Company) is a high-end brand in Schaffhausen, Switzerland. Although the company has historic roots back to 1868, the business is now part of the Richemont Group. Probably their most luxurious and exclusive timepiece to date is the phenomenal Ingenieur Constant-Force Tourbillon IW5900. This watch has a well-proportioned platinum and ceramic case measuring 46 mm × 14 mm. What makes this timepiece so outstanding is its exceptionally complex textured black dial that perfectly showcases the majestic rotating tourbillon carriage (at nine o'clock). Other features include double moon phase and power reserve indications. At the heart of the watch is a 43-jewel mechanical hand-winding movement.

Duomètre Sphérotourbillon, 75. Switzerland

Jaeger LeCoultre Duomètre Sphérotourbillon

In the world of horology, Jaeger LeCoultre is renowned for its exquisite range of complicated mechanical timepieces. In 1833, self-taught watchmaker Antoine LeCoultre established the business in Le Sentier, Switzerland. Today, the business is part of the luxury goods giant Richemont SA. In 2012, they released their award winning (public prize at the 5th edition of Munichtime) Duomètre Sphérotourbillon. With a classically proportioned 18-karat pink gold case measuring 42 mm × 14.10 mm, this watch is designed for the connoisseur. What makes this timepiece so impressive is the meticulous white crystalline grained dial with contrasting 18-karat pink gold hands and numerals. Other features include a large aperture (at nine o'clock) displaying the formidable rotating tourbillon carriage. Powering the watch is a 55-jewel hand-winding movement containing 460 separate parts.

The Charming Bird, 28. Switzerland

Jaquet Droz
The Charming Bird

Jaquet Droz is widely acknowledged in the world of horology as a watchmaker of distinction. Although the brand has historical roots dating to 1738, the Swatch Group now owns the business. At Baselworld 2013 they unveiled probably their most complicated watch to date, The Charming Bird. With a substantial 18-karat white gold case measuring 47 mm × 15.75 mm, the watch is designed to make a striking statement. What makes this timepiece so glorious is the multi-layered dial with miniature singing bird indication; this sublime three-dimensional characteristic is both beautiful and captivating. Other features include a sub counter displaying hours/minutes and an ornate top-mounted crown. Beneath the luxurious façade lies a Swiss-made 38-jewel self-winding mechanical movement.

Palace, 1. Switzerland

Jean Dunand Palace

Jean Dunand is a high-end contemporaryLe Locle, Switzerland. Specialist watchmaker Christophe Claret and entrepreneur Thierry Oulevay founded the company in 2003. Probably their most innovative creation to date is the sensational Palace. This watch is inspired by 'Art Deco' structures of the 1930's and has a titanium/white gold case measuring 48.2 x 49.9 mm x 16.65 mm. What makes the timepiece so magnificent is the bold 3-dimensional architectural dial. This feature delicately exposes the flying tourbillon mechanism and has cool modernist appearance. Other details include open worked hour/minute hands, GMT function and power reserve indication. Powering the watch is a 53-jewel hand-winding movement composed of 703 separate parts.

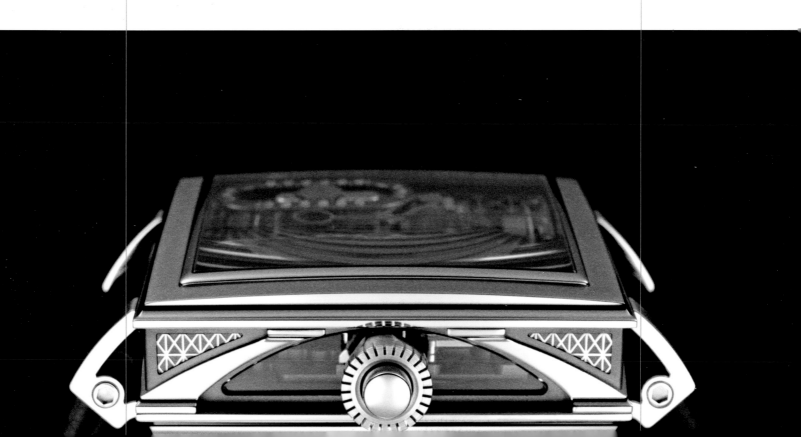

In Paris, 1. France

Jean-Baptiste Viot "In Paris"

Jean-Baptiste Viot is a specialist watchmaker situated in fashionable Paris, France. Prior to establishing his own brand he worked for companies like Patek Philippe, Brequet, Vacheron Constantin, and Blancpain. His aptly named "In Paris" is his first and only watch to date. The case, by modern standards, is relatively diminutive at only 38 mm × 10 mm. What makes this timepiece so amazing is the beautiful open-worked skeleton dial that perfectly exposes all elements of the meticulously hand-engraved mechanism. Other features include detachable lugs, three-dimensional steel hands, and a black chapter ring with contrasting gold markers. At the heart of the watch is a sophisticated manual winding movement.

GMR, 12. Switzerland

Kari Voutilainen GMR

Kari Voutilainen is a Finish watchmaker now residing in picturesque Môtiers, Switzerland. His brand goes under the trading name Voutilainen (Horlogerie d'Art) and was established in 2002. All of his wonderful watches are produced in his workshops, including the brilliant GMR. With a classical 39 mm 18-karat white gold case, this watch is designed to make a subtle statement. What makes this timepiece so refined is the beautiful hand-engraved solid silver dial; this incredible detail works in perfect harmony with the bespoke hour/minutes hands and large Roman numerals. Other features include a small GMT sub counter and retrograde power reserve indication. At the heart of the watch is a sophisticated 28-jewel manual winding mechanical movement.

2930, 30. USA

Keaton Myrick 2930

Keaton Myrick is a traditional watchmaker in Sisters (Deschutes County, Oregon). After fastidiously restoring many high-end mechanical watches for six years, Keaton decided to establish his own boutique brand. So far he has produced one exciting model called the 2930. This timepiece displays modest proportions and has a 42 mm 316L stainless steel case. What makes this watch so stylish is the hand-finished circular grained silver dial, giving the timepiece a contemporary appearance. Other details include delicate blued-steel hour/minute hands and a small second sub counter (at nine o'clock). Powering the watch is a bespoke hand-winding movement with German silver plates and bridges.

Red Gold Tourbillon, 1. Netherlands *Photos courtesy of Lucas de Peslouan*

Kees Englebarts
Red Gold Tourbillon

Kees Englebarts is a Dutch watchmaker based in Geneva, Switzerland. Before he established his own company he worked for Van Cleef & Arpels, Vacheron Constantin, Jaeger LeCoultre, and Philippe Dufour. Recently he unveiled a new interpretation of his popular Organic Tourbillon called the Red Gold Tourbillon. Dimensionally the watch has a well proportioned 18-Karat red gold case measuring 43 mm. What makes this timepiece so phenomenal is the exquisite hand-engraved skeleton dial with its bold and distinctive gothic appearance. Other features include sublime etched Mokume-Gane gold hour/minute hands and a majestic rotating tourbillon (at nine o'clock). Beneath the luxurious façade lies a Swiss-made 27-jewel twin barrel hand-winding movement.

CVDK Planetarium CKPT2225, 1. Netherlands

Klaauw Watches CVDK Planetarium CKPT2225

Christiaan van der Klaauw is a master watchmaker specializing in the production of fine astronomical mechanical watches. The company is based in Heerenveen, Netherlands, and celebrated its fortieth anniversary in 2014. The superb CVDK Planetarium is one of their more exclusive pieces. This watch displays modest proportions and has an extravagant 40 mm platinum case. What makes this timepiece so enticing is the stylish hand-decorated silver dial that displays the orbits of Mercury, Venus, Earth, Mars, Jupiter, and Saturn around the Sun. Other features include delicate hour/minute hands and a date complication (at twelve o'clock). Powering the watch is a self-winding 35-jewel twin barrel movement with a ninety-six-hour power reserve.

Lunokhod, 12. Russia

Konstantin Chaykin
Lunokhod

Konstantin Chaykin is a small innovative watchmaker in Moscow, Russia. Over the last few years he has become renowned for his unique and eclectic creations. The Lunokhod is one of his boldest designs and is a great example of his work. The watch exhibits massive proportions and measures 50 mm (excluding the crown). What makes this timepiece so eye catching is the distinctive wootz steel case and dial with its unique patterned texture that was created by master craftsmen. Other details include a three-dimensional spherical moon phase indication and skeletonized sub dial (at six o'clock) displaying hours/minutes. At the heart of the watch is a bespoke 31-jewel mechanical movement.

KudOktopus, 1. Germany

Kudoke KudOktopus

Kudoke is a small independent watchmaker from Germany specializing in the production of elegant bespoke watches. Stefan Kudoke is the brain behind the business. He has worked for companies like Glashütte Original, Breguet, Omega, and Blancpain. The KudOktopu is entirely hand made and a great example of his work. This watch is available in 18-karat gold or stainless steel and has a 42 mm diameter. What makes this timepiece so attractive is the exquisite engraved skeletonized dial with its beautiful rose gold/rhodium octopus with eight tentacles. Other fine details include tempered blue Breguet-style hour/minute hands and an ornate crown. Powering the watch is a 17-jewel Swiss-made mechanical hand-winding movement.

Albert von Sachsen, Germany

Lang & Heyne
Albert von Sachsen

Lang & Heyne is a high-end brand in the heart of Dresden, Germany; two passionate watchmakers (Marco Lang and Marco Heyne) founded the company. In partnership they have created many beautiful timepieces, including the fantastic Albert von Sachsen. With a luxurious 950 platinum case measuring 44 mm, the watch is designed for the connoisseur. What makes this timepiece so appealing is the understated minimalistic sunken white enamel dial that perfectly interacts with the black Roman numerals and chronograph timers. At the heart of the watch is a sophisticated 22-jewel mechanical hand-winding movement with a 46-hour power reserve.

Galet Micro-Rotor Platinum Limited Edition, 18. Switzerland

Laurent Ferrier Galet Classic Tourbillon Double Spiral

Laurent Ferrier is a high-end specialist watchmaker in the heart of Geneva, Switzerland. Interestingly, he began his career in motorsports and later established his own watch company in 2010. In 2012, he released a new limited edition version of his highly successful Galet Classic Tourbillon Double Spiral. This watch is constructed from stainless steel and has a classically sized case measuring 41 mm. What makes this timepiece so special is the exquisite hand-crafted 18-karat gold guilloché sunburst dial. This amazing feature compliments the teardrop-style white gold numerals. Other details include 18-karat gold "assegai shape" hour/minutes hands and a small second counter (at six o'clock). Powering the watch is a 23-jewel Swiss-made mechanical movement containing 188 components.

Oktopus Moon Tattoo, 59. England

Linde Werdelin Oktopus Moon Tattoo

Linde Werdelin is a small boutique watchmaker in London, England. Progressive designers Morten Linde and Jorn Werdelin established the company in 2002. Probably their most distinctive and complicated watch to date is the magnificent Oktopus Moon Tattoo, which displays generous proportions, measuring 44 mm × 46 mm × 15 mm. What makes this watch so striking is the meticulous hand-finished solid 18-karat red gold case. This amazing feature is constructed from nineteen components and has a wonderful engraved octopus. Other elements of the design include a refined skeleton dial with a complicated moon phase indication. At the heart of the watch is a Swiss-made mechanical self-winding movement with a forty-two-hour power reserve.

Derrick Gaz Tourbillon, 28. Switzerland

Louis Moinet SA Derrick Gaz Tourbillon

Louis Moinet SA is a high-end watchmaker that derives its name from the inventor of the first chronograph. The company was created by innovative designer Jean-Marie Schaller and is in Saint-Blaise, Switzerland. At Baselworld 2015 the brand unveiled one of their most exciting creations to date, called the Derrick Gaz Tourbillon. With an extravagant 18-karat white gold case measuring 47 mm × 14.10 mm, the watch is designed to make a striking statement. What makes this timepiece so wonderful is its stunning multi-layered dial: an architectural lacquered "Clous de Paris" engraved blue dial depicting a three-dimensional representation of an oil tower and pipelines. Powering the watch is an accomplished 39-jewel mechanical hand-winding tourbillon movement.

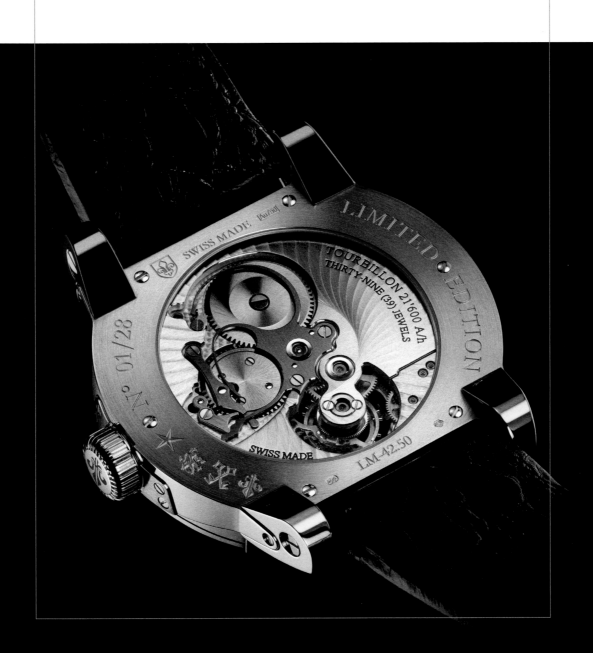

Half Time, 12. Switzerland

Ludovic Ballouard Half Time

Ludovic Ballouard is a French-born watchmaker who now resides in Satigny, Switzerland. Prior to establishing his own brand in 2009, he worked for companies like Frank Muller and FP Journe. All of his watches are fastidiously handcrafted, including the superb Half Time. This watch displays classical proportions and has a luxurious 950 platinum case measuring 41 mm × 11 mm. What makes this timepiece so interesting is the matte black dial with large contrasting white Roman numerals. Interestingly, hours are presented on a rotating disk (via a window located at twelve o'clock) and minutes are showcased in a retrograde format. Beneath the opulent façade lies a complicated 53-jewel mechanical hand-winding movement.

Frequential One F110, 25. Switzerland

Manufacture Contemporaine du Temps Frequential One F110

Manufacture Contemporaine du Temps (MCT) is an avant-garde watchmaker situated on the shores of Lake Neuchatel in Switzerland. The powerhouse behind the company is progressive designer François Candolfi. Since 2008, they have produced an exciting range of watches, including the distinctive Frequential One F110. Dimensionally the timepiece has a well-proportioned grade 5 titanium cushion-shaped case measuring 42 mm × 42 mm × 14 mm. What makes this watch so seductive is the bold open-worked black dial. This characteristic exposes elements of the mechanism and has an industrial appearance. Beneath the contemporary exterior lies a 33-jewel in-house-developed mechanical hand-winding movement.

Chapter One Tonneau Transparence Titanium, 11. USA

Maîtres du Temps Chapter One Tonneau Transparence Titanium

Maîtres du Temps is an experimental watch brand developed by Steven Holtzman. The essence of the company is to combine the talents of many master watchmakers like Kari Voutilainen, Peter Speake-Marin, Andreas Strehler, Christophe Claret, and Daniel Roth. A few years ago they created an exciting new model called the Chapter One Tonneau Transparence Titanium. This watch has a massive case measuring 62.60 mm × 45.90 mm × 18 mm. What makes this timepiece so incredible is the intricate handcrafted skeletonized dial. Functionally the watch features hours, minutes, chronograph timers, moon phase, and GMT indications. Powering the timepiece is a 53-jewel mechanical movement that contains 552 separate parts.

Opera, 4 a year. Switzerland

Manufacture Royale Opera

Manufacture Royale is a luxury Swiss watchmaker with roots dating to 1771. In 2010, the business was revived and is now owned by cousins David Gouten, Alexis Gouten, and Marc Gouten. Probably the most impressive and exclusive timepiece the company has created so far is the formidable Opera. It has a diameter measuring 50 mm. What makes this timepiece so extraordinary is the concertina case design that opens up to give the watch a whole new dynamic and was inspired by the design of the iconic Opera House in Sydney, Australia. Beneath the luxurious 18-karat gold façade lies a refined 29-jewel mechanical hand-winding tourbillon movement.

Tourbillon Prototype, 1. Switzerland

Marc Alfieri Tourbillon

Marc Alfieri is an accomplished designer situated in Marseille, France. Over the last few years he has specialized in the creation of products such as knives, wine glasses, fountain pens, and wristwatches. The Tourbillon is one of his latest and most exclusive timepieces. With a durable lightweight titanium case measuring 44 mm, the watch is well proportioned. What makes this timepiece so attractive is the superb handcrafted sterling silver dial that perfectly interacts with the modernistic hour/minute hands and large silver number "12." Other features include a moon phase indicator and large aperture (at six o'clock) displaying the rotating tourbillon carriage. At the heart of the watch is a refined manual winding movement with an eighty-hour power reserve.

Ka La Koa, 10. United States

Mark Carson Ka La Koa

Mark Carson is a talented independent watchmaker situated in idyllic Honolulu, Hawaii. As well as producing his own range of distinctive timepieces, he has also designed watches with Richard Paige. The Ka La Koa is one of the most innovative and unique timepieces he has produced to date. With a massive case measuring 55 mm × 47 mm (including the lugs), the watch is designed to make a bold statement. What makes this watch so appealing is the beautiful hand-crafted solid Koa wooden dial. Other striking features include bespoke ribbon-shaped lugs, central second hand disc indication, and a domed crystal lens. Powering the watch is a 25-jewel Swiss-made self-winding ETA 2824-2 movement.

JJJ J02, 3. Switzerland

Marc Jenni JJJ J02

Marc Jenni is a small specialist luxury watchmaker in Zurich, Switzerland. Prior to establishing his own brand he worked for the American jeweler Tiffany & Co. and Paul Gerber. The JJJ J02 is a marvelous creation inspired by an antique pocket watch created by Johan Jakob Jenny. Dimensionally the watch has a well-proportioned 44 mm 18-karat white gold case. What makes this watch so original is the black metalized sapphire crystal dial with contrasting Superluminova treated markers. Functionally the watch features hours, minutes, seconds, day/date, and planet indications. Beneath the elegant façade lies a bespoke 23-jewel Swiss-made mechanical self-winding movement.

Wadokei Revision, 1. Japan

Masahiro Kikuno
"Wadokei Revision"

Masahiro Kikuno is a young independent watchmaker in Hokkaido, Japan. In 2011, he became a member of the highly prestigious AHCI (Académie Horlogère des Créateurs Indépendants). The "Wadokei Revision" was released in 2015, and is a new interpretation of his 2011 model called the Temporal Hour Watch. With a modest oxidized bronze and stainless steel case measuring only 42 mm × 34 mm, the timepiece displays subtle proportions. What makes this watch so striking is the multi-layered skeletonized dial. Other exquisite details include hand-engraved indexes (by Keiji Kanagawa) and delicate violet hour/minute hands. At the heart of the watch is a 21-jewel mechanical hand-winding movement.

Masterpiece Gravity "40th anniversary",
40. Switzerland

Maurice Lacroix Masterpiece Gravity "40th Anniversary"

Maurice Lacroix is a luxury watchmaker situated in the heart of Zurich, Switzerland. In 2015, the company celebrated its fortieth anniversary and is now under the helm of CEO Stéphane Waser. One of their most impressive watches (of recent times) is the Masterpiece Gravity. The watch is classically proportioned and has a 43 mm 316L stainless steel case. What makes this timepiece really stand out is the striking partially skeletonized lacquered dial giving the watch a three-dimensional architectural appearance. Powering the watch is a highly accomplished Swiss-made mechanical self-winding movement. This calibre comprises 35 jewels and oscillates at a frequency of 18,000 vibrations per hour (2.5 Hz).

Horological Machine No°6, 18. Switzerland

MB & F Horological Machine No°6

MB & F (Maximilian Büsser & Friends) is a high-end avant-garde watchmaker situated in the heart of Geneva, Switzerland. The company operates in a collaborative manner similar to Maîtres du Temps and harnesses the talents of a range of different craftsmen. Recently the company released a second version of the successful Horological Machine No°6 constructed from 5N+ red gold. It measures 49.5 mm × 52.3 mm × 20.4 mm. What makes this timepiece so extraordinary is its perfectly sculpted futuristic case with ten individual sapphire crystal windows, allowing the recipient to view the mechanism and time in a completely unique way. Powering the watch is a complicated 68-jewel self-winding movement containing 475 parts.

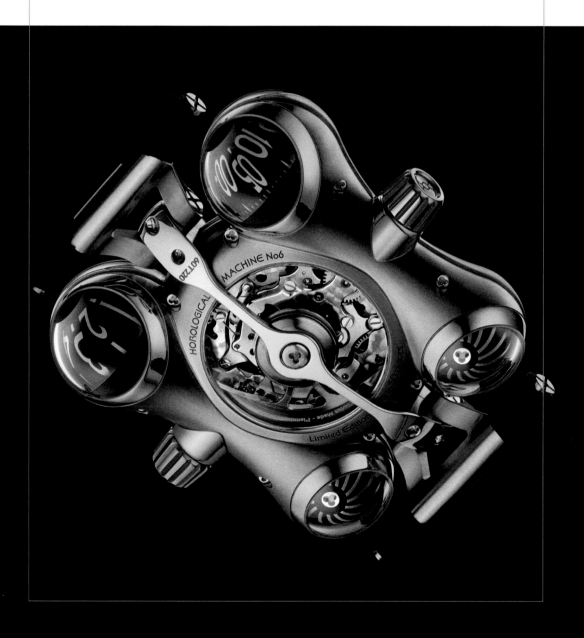

Tuscar - One in Ten, 10. Ireland

McGonigle Tuscar - One in Ten

McGonigle is a luxury small independent watchmaker situated in picturesque County Westmeath, Ireland. Dynamic brothers John and Stephen McGonigle established the company in 2007. The Tuscar - One in Ten is a marvelous looking watch and a great example of their talents. With an 18-karat white gold case measuring 43 mm, the watch is designed for the discerning. What makes this timepiece so refined is the minimalistic skeleton dial that exposes the intricate mechanical aspects of the watch. Other details include untreated silver bridges and hand-polished blued-steel hour/minute hands with white gold arrowheads. At the heart of the watch is a sophisticated 31-jewel manual winding movement.

Quattro Valvole CCM Brembo, 30. Italy

Meccaniche Veloci Quattro Valvole CCM Brembo

Meccaniche Veloci is a progressive Italian watchmaker that now has its headquarters in Geneva, Switzerland. In 2015, the entrepreneurial Cesare Cerito bought the business from Italian jeweler Cielo Venezi 1270. Probably the most unusual and impressive watch the company has produced so far is the sensational Quattro Valvole CCM Brembo. The timepiece measures 50 mm × 16 mm (excluding the crowns). What makes this watch so special is the handcrafted case constructed from Brembo carbon ceramic brake pads; this incredible material acts as a perfect backdrop for four separate dials. Beneath the robust exterior lie four individual 25-jewel automatic ETA 2761 mechanical movements.

Timeburner Chrome Rider ME2, 99. Switzerland

Miki Eleta Timeburner Chrome Rider ME2

Miki Eleta is a specialist craftsman that manufactures a range of exclusive watches and clocks. Originally Mika was born in Visegrad (Bosnia and Herzegovina), then relocated to Switzerland in 1973. In 2015, he unveiled a radical watch at Baselworld called the Timeburner Chrome Rider ME2, which has a 48 mm diameter. What makes this timepiece so distinctive is the unique case design constructed from titanium and bronze. The design is based on the nineteenth-century internal combustion engine and time is displayed in an unconventional manner: hours are presented on a rotating disc and minutes via a linear piston indication. At the heart of the watch is a modified (by Marc Jenni) Unitas 6497-1 mechanical hand-winding movement.

Art Piece One, 1. Slovakia

Molnár Fábry Art Piece One

Molnár Fábry is a small bespoke watchmaker situated in the beautiful city of Banská Bystrica, in Slovenia. The company was founded in 2005 by specialist jewelers Michal Molnar and Igor Fabry. One of their more interesting designs is the elegant Art Piece One. This watch has a classical-size 316L stainless steel case measuring 42 mm. What makes this timepiece so delightful is the sublime hand-engraved floral open-heart dial. This exquisite characteristic gives the watch a really sophisticated and stylish appearance. Other features include a luxurious 18-karat gold chapter ring and blued-steel hour/minute hands. Beneath the elegant façade lies a Swiss-made 17-jewel Unitas 6497-1 mechanical hand-winding movement.

Tourbillon Bi-Cylindrique, 25. Germany

Montblanc Tourbillon Bi-Cylindrique

Montblanc is a German luxury goods company that specializes in the production of fine jewelery, writing instruments, and timepieces. Even though the business was originally established in 1906, it is now part of the Richemont Group. The Tourbillon Bi-Cylindrique is one of the most complicated and exclusive timepieces they have ever produced. With an elegant 18-karat white gold case measuring 47 mm × 44 mm, the watch is designed for the connoisseur. What makes this creation so unique is the open heart dial exposing the (world's first) tourbillon with double cylindrical balance springs. Other features include a stylish silver sub dial with contrasting black Roman numerals. At the heart of the watch is a sophisticated mechanical hand-winding movement comprising 284 parts.

MIL N°7104 Timothy John, 39. Hong Kong

Montres-Militaire MIL N°7104
Timothy John

Within a relatively short space of time Montres-Militaire has established itself as a quality watchmaker. After three years of extensive research and development Hong Kong businessman Angus Yang eventually founded the company in 2013. Their most interesting and exclusive model so far is the wonderful MIL N°7104 Timothy John. This watch has a generously proportioned solid bronze case measuring 47 mm. What makes this timepiece so impressive is the meticulously hand-painted dial executed by South Australian artist Timothy John depicting an image of a skull. Other details include a rotating bezel and sapphire crystal lens. Powering the watch is a Swiss-made 17-jewel Unitas 6497-1 mechanical hand-winding movement.

Benu Tourbillon, 50. Germany

Moritz Grossmann
Benu Tourbillon

Moritz Grossmann is a small independent brand situated in the heart of Glashütte, Germany. Although Carl Moritz Grossmann originally founded the business in 1826, it is now under the helm of watchmaker Christine Hutter. The Benu Tourbillon is one of their most exclusive models and is limited to fifty pieces worldwide. With a luxurious 18-karat gold case measuring 44.5 mm × 13.8 mm, the watch is designed to make a striking statement. What makes this timepiece so enticing is the exquisite solid silver open-heart dial. This characteristic perfectly showcases the majestic rotating tourbillon. Other features include two sub counters displaying hours/seconds and a large central minute hand. Beneath the opulent façade lies an accomplished mechanical hand-winding movement composed of 245 individual parts.

Trio Retrograde Copper Dial, 5 a year. Germany

Nienaber Trio Retrograde Version 1

Nienaber-Uhren is a small independent watch and clockmaker situated in picturesque Bünde, Germany. Rainer Nienaber originally established the company in 1984. The Trio Retrograde Version 1 is one of their latest and most distinctive models. Dimensionally the watch has a well-proportioned classical 316L stainless steel case measuring 44 mm × 12 mm. What makes this timepiece so eye catching is the beautifully handcrafted copper color dial with contrasting black numerals and markers. Hours and seconds are displayed on two small sub counters and minutes via a large central hand. At the heart of the watch is a modified Swiss-made 17-jewel Unitas 6497-1 mechanical hand-winding movement.

Quickindicator Version 1, 97. Switzerland

Nord Zeitmaschine
Quickindicator

Nord Zeitmaschine is a boutique watchmaker established by Daniel Nebel situated in the heart of Büsserach, Switzerland. Over the last seventeen years the brand has become synonymous with exciting, unique mechanical watches. Their marvelous Quickindicator is the company's latest model and was unveiled at Baselworld 2013. The watch is classically proportioned and has a case measuring 44.3 mm × 15.6 mm. What makes this watch so extraordinary is its highly complicated multi-layered dial. Effectively the minute hand travels on three overlapping tracks and makes three revolutions per hour. Powering the watch is a modified 25-jewel ETA 2824-2 mechanical self-winding movement.

Moon Phase, 1. Switzerland

Ochs und Junior
Moon Phase

Ochs und Junior is a small specialist watchmaker situated in Lucerne, Switzerland. The company only produces 150 timepieces a year and they sell exclusively from their own website. One of their most popular designs is the phenomenal Moon Phase watch. This timepiece is available in a range of different materials and case sizes. What makes these watches so unique is they can be customized to the client's exact specifications. Recent dials have been constructed from rusty iron, copper, and gold leaf. Other features include a highly complicated moon phase indication devised by Ludwig Oechslin. Powering the watch is a modified Swiss-made ETA 2824-2 25-jewel mechanical self-winding movement.

Speed F1, 33. Switzerland

Ollivier Savéo Speed F1

Ollivier Savéo is an exclusive watchmaker situated in the heart of Geneva, Switzerland. Specialist jeweler and artist Ollivier Savelli founded the company in 2014. All of his creations are a delight to the eye, including his wonderful Speed F1. The watch has a well-proportioned case measuring 44 mm × 41 mm × 14 mm, and is constructed from lightweight forged carbon and 18-karat white gold. What makes this timepiece so impressive is the open-worked skeletonized façade inspired by the modern architecture of luxury cars. Other features include an oversize industrial-style crown and vibrant red hour/minute hands. At the heart of the watch is a Swiss-made 26-jewel mechanical automatic movement.

Pocket Watch Tourbillon
GMT Ceramica, 50.
Switzerland

Panerai Pocket Watch Tourbillon GMT Ceramica

Panerai is large luxury watchmaker situated in the heart of Milan, Italy. Although Giovanni Panerai originally established the business in 1860, the company is now a subsidiary of the Richemont Group. The Pocket Watch Tourbillon GMT Ceramica is probably their most complicated and exclusive creation to date. With a large scratch-resistant matte black ceramic case measuring 59 mm, the watch is designed to attract attention. What makes the timepiece so appealing is its sublime hand-decorated skeletonized dial that delicately exposes various mechanical elements of the watch, including the majestic rotating tourbillon. Beneath the cool exterior lies a Swiss-made 31-jewel movement with a six-day power reserve.

Polaris, 1. Australia/USA

Paolo Mathai Polaris

Paolo Mathai is an experimental creative platform established by Frank Heydrich and myself (Steve Huyton). Originally I came up with a detailed drawing based on a famous clock design by renowned 20th Century industrial designer George Nelson. Frank then constructed a unique timepiece called the Polaris. The watch has a Massive grade 5 titanium case measuring 53mm x 20mm. What makes this timepiece so unusual is the 'Art Deco' inspired skeletonized dial with three-dimensional semi precious stone spherical markers. Other features include bespoke open worked aluminum hour/minute hands and an oversize sculpted crown. Beneath the durable exterior lies a Swiss made 17-jewel Unitas 6497-1 mechanical hand-winding movement.

Bugatti Super Sport, 30. Switzerland

Parmigiani Fleurier Bugatti Super Sport

Parmigiani Fleurier is synonymous with its exquisite range of extravagant in-house manufactured timepieces. The brand was established in 1996 and their headquarters is in Fleurier, Switzerland. One of their most impressive creations so far is the fabulous Bugatti Super Sport. This incredible watch has a large 18-karat gold case measuring 36.3 mm × 50.5 mm × 23.3 mm and was inspired by the legendary sports car of the same name. What makes this timepiece so astounding is the striking three-dimensional skeletonized façade, enabling the recipient to view mechanical aspects of the watch via two sapphire windows. Powering the timepiece is a 40-jewel manual winding movement with an impressive ten-day power reserve.

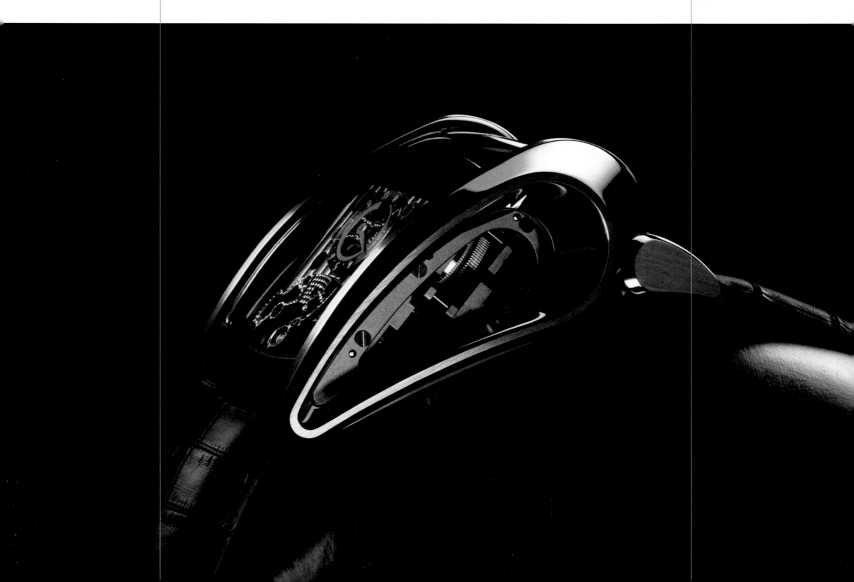

Sky Moon Tourbillon 6002G, 1. Switzerland

Patek Philippe
Sky Moon Tourbillon

Patek Philippe is widely regarded as one of the world's most prestigious watchmakers. Antoni Patek and Adrien Phillipe founded the company in 1851. Presently, the company employs over 2,000 employees and has its headquarters in Plan-les-Ouates, Switzerland. The Sky Moon Tourbillon is one of their most complicated timepieces and has a hand-engraved 18-karat white gold case measuring 42.8 mm × 16.25 mm. What makes this watch so extraordinary is its sublime blue enamel/gold dial with gold applied numerals and champlevé railway-track scale. The timepiece also has an impressive list of features, including hours, minutes, minute repeater, perpetual calendar, and moon phase indication. Beneath the luxurious façade lies a sophisticated mechanical hand-winding movement containing 705 individual parts.

Model 33, 25. Switzerland

Paul Gerber Model 33

Paul Gerber is a specialist watchmaker situated in the heart of Zurich, Switzerland. Among his many achievements he is credited (by the *Guinness Book of World Records*) for creating the world's most complicated timepiece. The Model 33 is a beautifully handcrafted watch that perfectly showcases his talents. With a luxurious tonneau case (available in 18-karat gold or platinum), the watch is designed for the discerning. What makes this watch so appealing is the sublime Guilloché dial with a three-dimensional spherical diamond moon phase indication (at eleven o'clock). Other features include raised 18-karat gold indexes and delicate open-worked blued-steel hour/minute hands. Powering the watch is a refined 18-jewel mechanical hand-winding movement.

Turbine Limited Edition Tourbillon A1077/1, 20. Switzerland

Perrelet SA Turbine Limited Edition Tourbillon A1077/1

Perrelet SA is an innovative watchmaker situated in historical Bienne, Switzerland. The company has roots dating to 1729 and was founded by Abraham-Louis Perrelet. In 2014, the brand unveiled one their most exclusive and complicated timepieces, the Turbine Limited Edition Turbillon A1077/1. The watch has a generously proportioned 316L stainless steel case measuring 46 mm × 13.40 mm. What makes this timepiece so enticing is its extraordinary sapphire skeleton dial that exposes the rotating tourbillon and ten-blade turbine. Other features include large bold numerals and stylized hour/minute hands. At the heart of the watch is a 27-jewel in-house mechanical self-winding movement.

Grande Sonnerie, 6. Switzerland

Philippe Dufour
Grande Sonnerie

Philippe Dufour is a highly distinguished watchmaker situated in Le Solliat, Switzerland. During his impressive career he has worked for prestigious companies like Jaeger-le-Coultre, Gerald Genta, and Audemars Piguet. Probably his most distinctive watch is the phenomenal Grande Sonnerie. The watch displays classical proportions and has an opulent 18-karat white gold case measuring 41 mm. What makes this timepiece so stunning is the handcrafted white enamel dial that works in perfect harmony with the large black Roman numerals. Other features include a small second counter (at six o'clock) and blued steel moon-style hour/minute hands. Powering the watch is a sophisticated 35-jewel mechanical hand-winding movement.

Prokop & Brož Frantisek Kupka Salon d'Automne-Paris 1912

Prokop & Brož is a luxury watchmaker situated in beautiful Praha, Czech Republic. Dynamic entrepreneurs Jan Prokop and Martin Brož established the company in 2012. The Frantisek Kupka Salon d'Automne-Paris 1912 was unveiled in 2012 and is the company's most complicated timepiece to date. With an opulent 14-karat white gold case measuring 44 mm, the watch is designed for the aficionado. What makes this watch so stylish is its beautiful white dial with dual retrograde display, giving the timepiece a delightfully charming appearance. Other features include patented asymmetrical steel lugs and an ornate 14-karat white gold crown. Powering the watch is a sophisticated mechanical hand-winding movement.

Torpedo, 1. France

Ralf Tech Torpedo 2015

Ralf Tech is a small independent watchmaker situated in La Garenne Colombes (Paris), France. The company is owned by Frank Huyghe and specializes in the production of mechanical dive watches. At Baselworld 2015 they unveiled their most distinctive and exclusive timepiece, the Torpedo 2015. With an oversized 316L stainless steel case measuring 47.5 mm, the watch is sure to make a bold statement. What makes this timepiece so interesting is the supreme three-dimensional façade inspired by an elusive Spanish C3 submarine; the dial perfectly replicates the back of a torpedo tube and has a really cool industrial appearance. Powering the watch is a Swiss-made 24-jewel self winding movement.

Raymond Weil Nabucco Cello Tourbillon

Raymond Weil is a luxury goods company based in the heart of Geneva, Switzerland. The business was originally established in 1976, and is now under the helm of Elie Berheim. One of their most extravagant timepieces is the sensational Nabucco Cello Tourbillon. This watch has a generously proportioned steel, titanium, and carbon case measuring 46.5 mm × 12.95 mm. What makes this timepiece so outstanding is its beautifully crafted open-worked cello string black dial that delicately exposes mechanical elements of the watch. Other features include stylized hour/minute hands and a large rotating tourbillon carriage. Beneath the striking exterior lies a sophisticated hand-winding movement with a 105-hour power reserve.

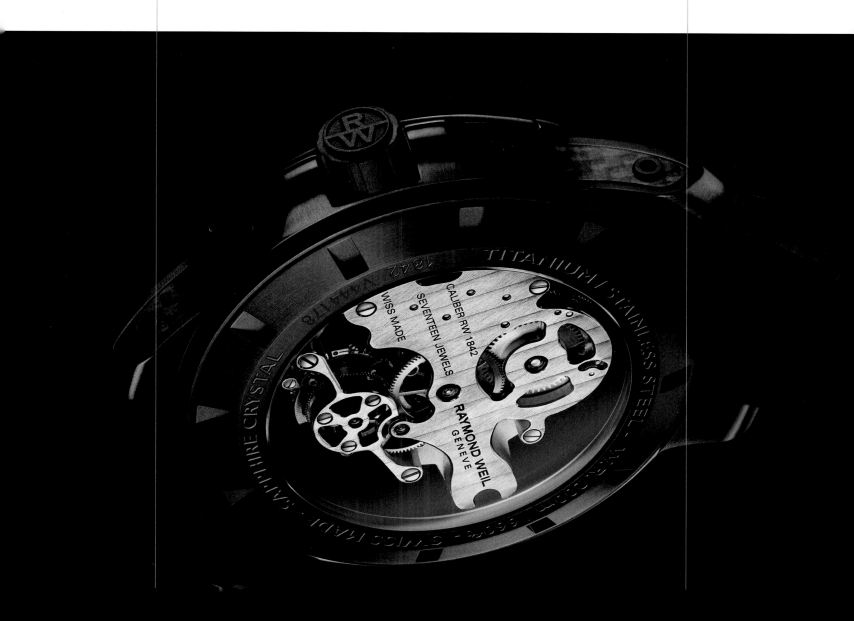

Gotham, 25. Switzerland

Rebellion T1000 Gotham

Rebellion is a high-end avant-garde watchmaker based in Lonay, on the banks of Lake Geneva, Switzerland. Within a relatively short space of time the company has produced a range of exciting timepieces. The T1000 Gotham is one of their most distinctive and ambitious creations to date, with a diameter measuring 52.5 mm. What makes this timepiece so awesome is its futuristic architectural titanium façade, allowing the recipient to view the mechanism from many different aspects. Time is ingeniously displayed on two rotating vertical barrels. At the heart of the watch is an extremely complicated hand-winding movement with a staggering 1,000-hour power reserve.

Type 3, 50. Belgium

Ressence Type 3

Ressenc+e is a Belgium-based watch label established by industrial designer Benoit Mintiens. The company derived its unusual name by combining the words *renaissance* and *essence*. Their latest watch, the Type 3, was released in 2013. The timepiece has a well-proportioned lightweight (eighty grams) Sapphire crystal and is made of grade 5 titanium; it measures 44 mm × 15 mm. What makes this timepiece so phenomenal is its unique ultra-contemporary liquid-filled façade. Impressively the watch is also devoid of a crown and conventional hands. Information is transmitted from the movement to dial via micro-magnetic fields. Beneath the futuristic exterior lies a Swiss-made 25-jewel automatic mechanical movement with an additional patented 57-jewel module.

Richard Mille RM 56-02 Filipe Massa Sapphire

The name Richard Mille is renowned in the watch industry for its range of exceptionally high quality modernistic timepieces. The company is also considered an innovator because of its use of experimental lightweight materials. Recently the brand unveiled an exciting new watch called the RM 56-02 Filipe Massa Sapphire. With imposing proportions (50.50 mm × 42.70 mm × 19.25 mm), this watch is designed to make a bold statement. What makes this watch so extraordinary is the case is completely composed of sapphire crystal, which is extremely scratch resistant and has a hardness of 1,800 Vickers. It also has a wonderful skeletonized dial that perfectly exposes all the mechanical elements of the watch. Beneath the transparent façade lies a complicated Swiss-made hand-finished movement.

Persepolis 202/2 Blue Xerxes, 50. United States

Ritmo Mvndo Perspolis 202/2 Blue Xerxes

Ritmo Mvndo is an exciting watch brand situated in glamorous Los Angeles, California. Charismatic business owner Ali Sotani is a watch industry veteran and has sold luxurious pieces to celebrities including Michael Jackson. The Persopolis 202/2 Blue Xerxes is one of their more distinctive models and is limited to only fifty pieces. It has a diameter measuring 52.5 mm. What makes this timepiece so unique is the phenomenal orbital 316L stainless steel rotating case, allowing the recipient to alternate easily between two different time zones. At the heart of the watch are two Swiss-made 26-jewel Selita SW200 mechanical automatic movements.

Creative Skeleton Flying Tourbillon,
28. Switzerland

Roger Dubuis Creative Skeleton Flying Tourbillon

Roger Dubuis is a high-end watchmaker based in the heart of Geneva, Switzerland. Although Carlos Dias and Roger Dubuis originally founded the company, it is now part of the Richemont Group. The Creative Skeleton Flying Tourbillon is one of their most exclusive models and was unveiled at SIHH (Salon International de la Haute Horlogerie) 2015. Dimensionally the watch displays modest proportions and has an elegant 18-karat pink gold case (set with brilliant cut diamonds) measuring 42 mm. What makes this timepiece so extraordinary is the decorative floral skeletonized dial, giving the watch a striking and luxurious appearance. Other features include delicate open-worked hour/minute hands and a large exposed flying tourbillon. At the heart of the watch is a sophisticated mechanical hand-winding movement.

Red Robin, 50. England

Robert Loomes Red Robin

Robert Loomes is a fine traditional watchmaker situated in the heart of Stamford, England. Since 1654, the company has been producing a select range of handcrafted timepieces. The Red Robin is a beautiful timepiece that perfectly illustrates their enormous skill set. With a modest 18-karat gold case measuring 39 mm, the watch is designed to make a subtle statement. What makes this timepiece so elegant is the white frosted dial with contrasting black Roman numerals, giving the watch a top quality, classical appearance. As these timepieces are made to order, every timepiece will have its own unique characteristics. Powering the watch is a historical English mechanical hand-winding movement dating back to the 1950s.

Open Dial, made to order. England

Roger Smith Open Dial

Roger Smith is a talented independent brand based on the Isle of Man. Roger attended the Manchester School of Horology and was inspired by the works of legendary watchmaker Dr. George Daniels. The Open Dial is one of his most distinctive models and was originally released in 2010. Dimensionally the watch displays classical proportions and has a 40 mm diameter. What makes this timepiece so outstanding is its hand-finished multi-layered skeleton dial that showcases all of the intricate mechanical components of the watch. Other exquisite details include delicate hour/minute hands, a small second counter, and a retrograde power reserve indication. Beneath the luxurious 18-karat white gold exterior lies a complicated hand-winding movement.

Logical One Secret Kakau Höfke, 1. Switzerland

Romain Gauthier Logical One Secret Kakau Höfke

Romain Gauthier is a high-end watchmaker situated in picturesque Le Sentier (Vallée de Joux), Switzerland. Prior to establishing his own company in 2007, Romain worked as a machine programmer/operator at a renowned horological parts manufacturer. The Logical One Secret Kakau Höfke is probably his most distinctive timepiece to date. This watch has a classically sized luxurious 18-karat white gold case measuring 43 mm × 14.2 mm. What makes the timepiece so astounding is its beautifully handcrafted façade inspired by the works of modernist artist Kakau Höfke. This unique feature is composed of 352 individual jade and agate (0.5 mm thin) tiles. At the heart of the timepiece is a patented 71-jewel (chain and fusée style) constant force mechanical movement.

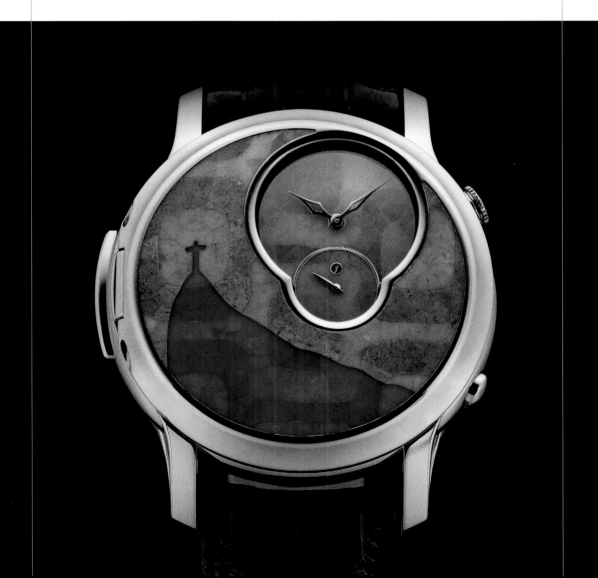

Légende Tourbillon, 10. Switzerland

Roshan Martin Haute Horlogerie SA
The Légende Tourbillon

Roshan Martin Haute Horlogerie SA is a high-end luxury watchmaker loacted in Montreux, Canton de Vaud, Switzerland. Prior to establishing his own brand Roshan worked for Jacob & Co and Audemars Piguet. The Légende Tourbillon was unveiled in 2014 at the Grand Prix d'Horlogerie de Genève (GPHG). This watch has a diameter of 43.5 mm × 5.7 mm and is constructed from lightweight titanium. What makes this watch so amazing is its beautiful multi-layered hand-engraved enamel dial that showcases all the brilliant mechanics of the watch, including the rotating tourbillon. At the heart of the watch is a super-slim (2.8 mm) 22-jewel mechanical hand-winding movement.

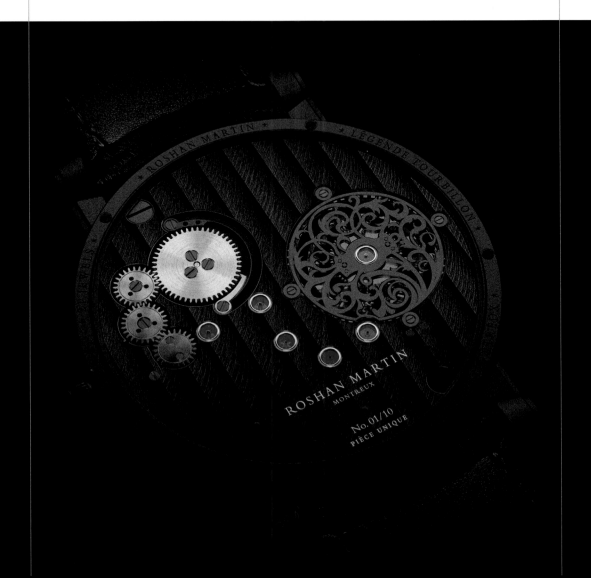

Duo Face Spaceview, 1. United States

RPaige Watch Duo Face Spaceview

RPaige is a small independent watch company situated in idyllic Honolulu, Hawaii. After running a successful chain of retail stores Richard Paige decided to launch his own brand. The Duo Face Spaceview is part of his latest collection and is a unique 1/1 piece. With a polished steel case measuring 44 mm × 57 mm × 12 mm, this watch is designed to make a bold statement. What makes this timepiece so appealing is its partially skeletonized black dial exposing mechanical elements of the watch, which has a striking industrial appearance. Other features include slim black Cathedral-style hands and a small second sub counter (at nine o'clock). Beneath the elegant exterior lies a vintage American hand-winding movement (from Elgin) dating to 1908.

Harmonious Oscillator, 50. Switzerland

Rudis Sylva Harmonious Oscillator

Rudis Sylva is a high-end contemporary watchmaker situated in Les Bois, Switzerland. The dynamic and entrepreneurial Jacky Epitaux established the company in 2007. So far they have only produced one exclusive model, the Harmonious Oscillator. This watch has a 44 mm × 14.3 mm case available in either 18-karat gold or lightweight titanium. What makes this timepiece so fantastic is its handcrafted skeletonized façade that perfectly showcases the brilliant mechanics of the watch. Other details include an offset black Guilloché grand feu enamel dial with contrasting red Roman numerals. Beneath the stylish exterior lies a bespoke hand-winding movement devised by master craftsman Mika Rissanen.

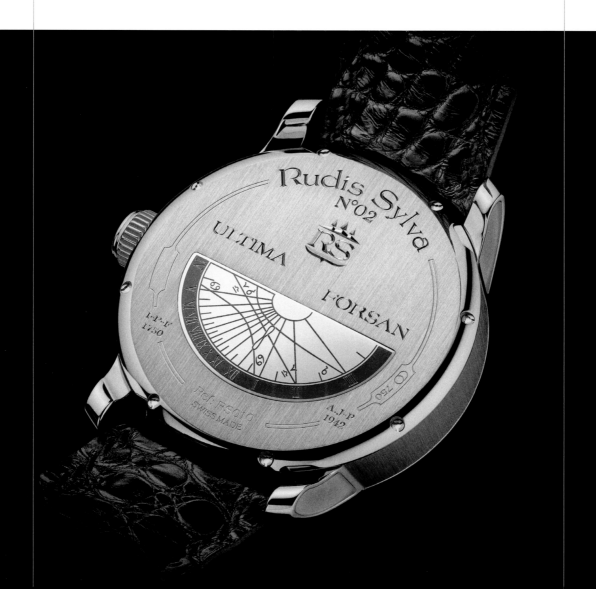

Sarpaneva Supernova

Sarpaneva is a small boutique watchmaker situated in vibrant Helsinki, Finland. As well as producing his own timepieces, Stepan Sarpaneva has also collaborated with brands like MB & F (on the Moonmachine). One of his most impressive timepieces to date is the Supernova. This watch is constructed from Stavax ESR hardened stainless steel and measures 40 mm × 11.5 mm. What makes this watch so exquisite is its phenomenal multi-layered open-worked dial. All of the components (including the stylized hour/minute hands) have been meticulously handcrafted to the highest possible standard. At the heart of the watch is a modified 25-jewel Swiss-made ETA 2824-A2 mechanical self-winding movement.

Tree of Luck, 1. Germany

Schaumburg Watch Paleonhorologie

Schaumburg Watch is a small independent brand situated in Rinteln, Germany. The company was established in 1998, and is widely acknowledged as a fine watchmaker. One of their most distinctive timepieces is the Paleonhorologie, from the highly successful Unikatorium Handmade collection. This watch features classical proportions and has a 42 mm brushed steel case. What makes this timepiece so delightful is its intricate (bone pattern) skeletonized dial that is entirely hand-decorated and has a sublime organic appearance. The exquisite mechanism is also visible through the sapphire crystal exhibition case back. Powering the watch is a Swiss-made 17-jewel hand-winding movement.

Blacklamp Carbon, 101. England

Schofield Blacklamp Carbon

Schofield is a small artisan watch manufacturer based in the heart of Surrey, England. Passionate designer Giles Ellis is the creative powerhouse behind the company. Probably their most impressive and exclusive watch to date is the supreme Blacklamp Carbon. This watch displays modest case proportions and has a diameter measuring 44 mm. What makes this timepiece so distinctive is its amazing textured black carbon façade. This trademark registered material is called Morta˚, and every case is machined to the highest possible standards. Other features include a gloss black engraved dial with complementary applied numerals and a tritium gas light. Beneath the exterior lies a Swiss-made 17-jewel Unitas 6498-1 mechanical hand-winding movement.

The Kennin-ji Temple Masters Project, 1. Switzerland

Speake-Marin SA
The Kennin-ji Temple
Masters Project

Speake-Marin SA is a high-end watchmaker in Bursins, Switzerland. Prior to establishing his own brand Peter Speake-Marin collaborated with companies like Harry Winston, MB & F, and Maîtres du Temps. The Kennin-ji Temple Masters Project is a unique 1/1 piece (commissioned by a private collector) that took a year to produce. Dimensionally the watch displays classical proportions and has a diameter measuring 42 mm. What makes this timepiece so astonishing is the incredible amount of detail. The 18-karat white gold case and dial feature two meticulously engraved dragons executed by master craftsman Kees Englebarts. Beneath the wonderful façade lies a sophisticated 29-jewel mechanical hand-winding movement.

la Clémence, 6. Switzerland

Spero Lucem la Clémence

Spero Lucem is a luxury goods brand that produces an exciting range of high-end pens, knives, and wristwatches. The company is based in Geneva, Switzerland, and was established by Yvan Arpa and Caiyun Song. Probably their most complicated timepiece so far is the sensational la Clémence, which has an extravagant 18-kart red gold case measuring 44 mm. What makes this timepiece so outstanding is the beautiful open-worked partially skeletonized hand-engraved dial. Functionally the watch features a rotating minute tourbillon and minute repeater. Interestingly, every time the bell strikes the hands of the timepiece go absolutely crazy. Powering the watch is a bespoke 59-jewel mechanical manual winding movement (devised by Pierre Favre) containing 471 individual components.

Deep Blue, 1. Switzerland

Steenman Watches
Deep Blue

Dick Steenman is a specialist independent watchmaker situated in the heart of Geneva, Switzerland. As well as producing his own range of exquisite timepieces he has worked for companies like Piaget, Chaumet, and Van Cleef & Arpels. The Deep Blue is a perfect example of his skills and was inspired by the coral reef. The watch exhibits classical proportions and has a 42 mm 18-karat white gold case. What makes this timepiece so seductive is its opulent hand-engraved (by artist Anita Porchet) 3 mm thick 18-karat white gold and blue enamel dial, giving the watch a beautiful and refined appearance. At the heart of the watch is a restored vintage Lemania 8810 self-winding mechanical movement.

Nethuns, 99. Switzerland

Strom Prestige Swiss Timepieces SA Nethuns

Strom Prestige Swiss Timepieces SA is a small independent company in Nidau-Biel, Switzerland. Designer, watchmaker, and philosopher Daniel Strom is the brainchild behind the business. Recently he unveiled one of his most exciting timepieces to date called the Nethuns (named after the god of water in Etruscan mythology). This watch has a massive handmade Corinthium Aes (alloy of copper, gold, and silver) case measuring 56 mm × 50 mm. What makes this timepiece so formidable is its amazing steampunk-inspired gothic appearance. Interestingly, minutes are displayed by a central hand and the jumping hour via a small window (at six o'clock). Beneath the robust exterior lies a Swiss-made mechanical self-winding movement.

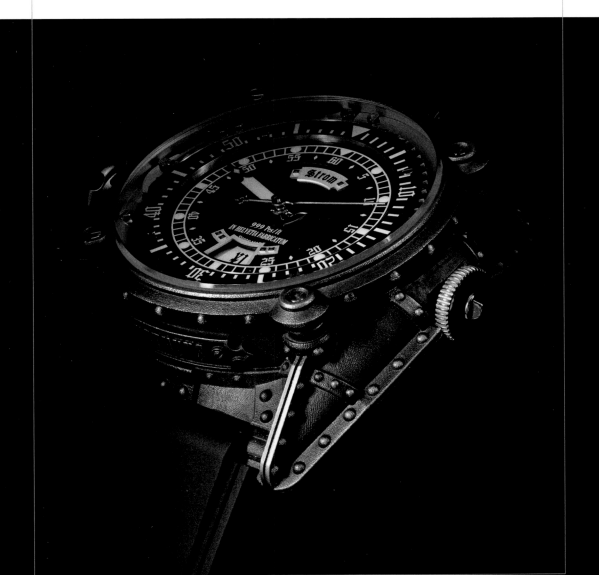

Carrera Mikropendulum, ca. 1. Swiss chrono[...]

Tag Heuer Carrera Mikropendulums

Tag Heuer is renowned in the world of horology for producing attractive and reliable Swiss-made timepieces. Although Edouard Heuer originally founded the business over 150 years ago, the company is now owned by LVMH (Louis Vuitton Moët Hennessy). Probably the most complicated and exclusive timepiece the brand has ever produced is the phenomenal Carrera Mikropendulums. The 47 mm case is constructed from a unique material (chrome and cobalt) that is usually used in the aviation industry. What makes this model so amazing is its distinctive multi-layered three-dimensional dial that perfectly exposes the two tourbillon pendulums and their solid rose gold bridges. At the heart of the watch is a patented 75-jewel mechanical movement containing 454 separate parts.

Nemo Captain, 1. Switzerland

Thomas Prescher
Nemo Captain

Thomas Prescher is an innovative watchmaker situated in idyllic Twann, Switzerland. Prior to establishing his own company Thomas worked for IWC and Audemars Piguet. One of his most distinctive pieces is the superb Nemo Captain. The watch is a classically proportioned 44 mm × 16.5 mm constructed from 18-karat gold and palladium. This timepiece has a wonderful art nouveau appearance inspired by the works of Jules Verne. What makes the watch so enticing is its large porthole showcasing the magnificent rotating tourbillon carriage. Other striking features include two nameplates and a discreet window (at five o'clock) displaying jumping hours. Beneath the refined façade is a 47-jewel mechanical hand-winding movement composed of 393 handcrafted parts.

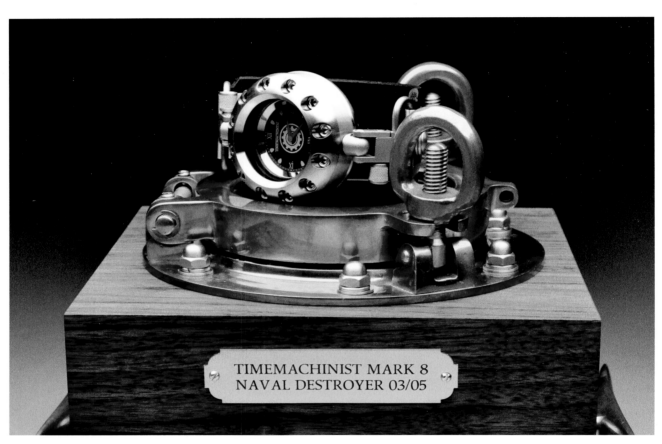

TIMEMACHINIST MARK 8
NAVAL DESTROYER 03/05

Mark 8, 5. United States

Timemachinist Mark 8

Timemachinist is a small contemporary watch company situated in Alaska. Enigmatic inventor and designer Cal Giordana is the creative powerhouse behind the brand. Over the last few years he has made a range of distinctive timepieces, including the brilliant Mark 8. This watch has a massive 55 mm × 28 mm bronze and steel case that weighs 368 grams. What makes this creation so unique is its brilliant industrial appearance. As these timepieces are completely handcrafted every one is slightly different. They are also presented in a wonderful solid black walnut and bronze bespoke case. Powering the watch is a Japanese Citizen Quartz Movement.

The Sound of History, 1. Germany

Torsten Nagengast
The Sound of History

Torsten Nagengast is a small independent watchmaker situated in Pforzheim (Black Forest), Germany. It was his passion for horology that stimulated him to establish his own brand. As well as producing a series of mainstream watches, he also creates unique pieces like The Sound of History. This timepiece delicately combines luxurious platinum with lightweight titanium and has a 43 mm diameter. What makes this watch so astounding is the sublime Guilloché skeletonized dial that works in perfect harmony with the intricate hour/minute hands and engraved chapter ring. Beneath the elegant façade lies a historical Patek Philippe minute repeater movement (originally made for Tiffanys in New York) dating to 1914.

U-1942, 29. Italy

U-Boat U-1942

Italian brand U-Boat is synonymous with the production of oversized handcrafted timepieces. Flamboyant Italo Fontana founded the business in 2000. A few years ago the company unveiled one of their largest and most exclusive pieces to date called the U-1942. This watch has a gigantic 64.4 mm diameter and has been worn in public many times by Arnold Schwarzenegger. What makes this timepiece so formidable is its enormous grade 5 titanium case with unique crown locking system. Other features include a black dial with contrasting large white numerals and a small second counter (at three o'clock). At the heart of the watch is a 17-jewel Unitas 6497-1 mechanical hand-winding movement.

FreakLab, 99. Switzerland

Ulysse Nardin FreakLab

Ulysse Nardin is a luxury watchmaker situated in picturesque Le Locle (Jura Mountains), Switzerland. Even though the business was originally established in 1846, the company is now under the helm of Patrik P. Hoffmann. One of their most exciting and latest offerings is the fabulous FreakLab. This watch has an extravagant 18-karat white gold case measuring 45 mm. What makes this timepiece so appealing is its stunning multi-layered black dial that perfectly showcases all the brilliant mechanical components of the watch. Other features include an innovative bezel-operated time and date setting device. Powering the watch is an accomplished manual-winding movement with a seven-day power reserve.

UR-1001 Titan, 8. Switzerland

Urwerk UR-1001 Titan

Urwerk is a small avant-garde watch brand in the heart of Geneva, Switzerland. Accomplished watchmaker Felix Baumgartner and chief designer Martin Frei established the company in 1997. At Baselworld 2015 they unveiled their most distinctive watch to date, the UR-1001 Titan. This incredible piece is probably the largest mechanical wristwatch in the world, measuring a whopping 106 mm × 62 mm × 23 mm. What makes this timepiece so exceptional is its complicated multi-layered dial that displays an impressive list of functions, including retrograde minutes, seconds, calendar, day/night indication, and an "Oil change" indicator. Beneath the robust exterior lies a sophisticated 51-jewel mechanical self-winding movement.

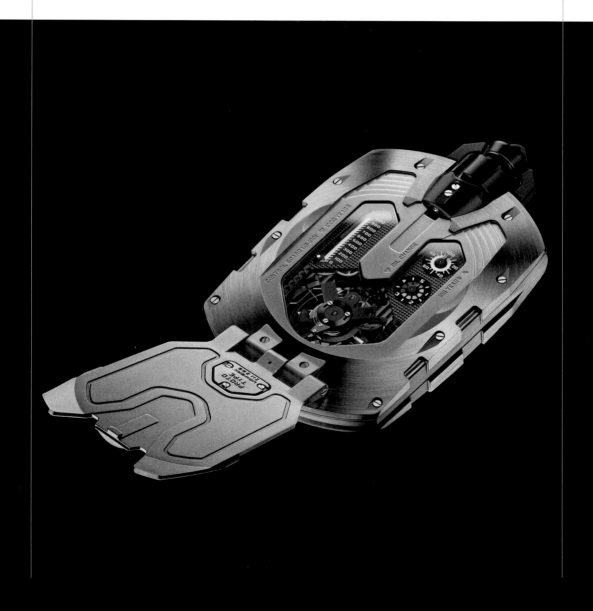

Malte Tourbillon Openworked, 10 a year. Switzerland

Vacheron Constantin Malte Tourbillon Openworked

Vacheron Constantin is widely regarded as one of the finest watchmakers in the industry. Although the company has roots dating to 1755, the Richemont Group now owns the business. One of their most impressive models to date is the sublime Malte Tourbillon Openworked. This amazing watch has an opulent platinum tonneau case measuring 48.24 mm × 38 mm × 12.73 mm. What makes this timepiece so wonderful is its sensational three-dimensional skeletonized dial that perfectly showcases all the brilliant mechanics of the watch. Other features include large white etched Roman numerals, a small sub counter displaying date indication, and a large exposed tourbillon carriage (at six o'clock). Powering the watch is a Hallmark of Geneva certified 27-jewel hand-winding movement.

Argentique, 36. Switzerland

Valbray Argentique

Valbray is a progressive young watch brand situated in Romanel sur Morges, Switzerland. Engineer Côme de Valbray and designer Olga Corsini established the business in 2009. A perfect example of their work is the supreme Argentique. Dimensionally the watch has a well-proportioned Grade 5 titanium and 316L stainless steel case measuring 46 mm. What makes this timepiece really stand out is the innovative and patented shutter system: sixteen fine blades (operated by the rotating bezel) allow the recipient to alternate between two futuristic dials. Other features include open-worked hour/minute hands and a sapphire crystal lens. At the heart of the watch is a Swiss-made 25-jewel mechanical self-winding movement.

Retrograde Wooden Watch, 10. Ukraine

Valerii Danevych Retrograde Wooden Watch

Valerii Danevych is a specialist independent artisan/craftsman in the heart of Kiev, Ukraine. Unlike many other watchmakers, he has no formal training in horology, just an extensive knowledge of joinery. His Retrograde Wooden Watch is one of the world's most unusual timepieces. What makes this piece so special is the handcrafted wooden 46 mm case constructed from canker (apple-tree, plum-tree), walnut, birch, Australian guaiacum, Crimea box, bamboo, and African bubinga. Each watch takes over 1,800 hours to produce and is completely unique. Even the skeletonized dial and mechanical flying tourbillon movement (188 separate components) are fabricated from this wonderful organic material.

Valour Sopwith Aviator, England

Valour Watch Company
Sopwith Aviator

Valour is a small independent watch brand situated in the county of Surrey, England. New Zealand-born engineer and designer Mark Daniel is the creative force behind the company. Currently they have only released one watch, the Sopwith Aviaitor. With a massive 316L stainless steel case that measures 54 mm, the timepiece is designed to make a bold statement. What makes this watch so special is its multi-layered façade inspired by a Sopwith Camel aircraft engine, giving the watch a unique industrial appearance. Other features include a cool matte black dial and bespoke hour/minute hands. Powering the watch is a customized Swiss-made Soprod A10-2 mechanical self-winding movement.

Deep Space, 30. Switzerland.

Vianney Halter Deep Space

Vianney Halter is an accomplished independent watchmaker based in idyllic Sainte-Croix, Switzerland. As well as producing his own range of timepieces, he has also collaborated with renowned brands like Harry Winston and Cabestan. One of his latest creations is the award winning (Grand Prix d'Horlogerie de Genève) Deep Space. This watch has an XL lightweight titanium case (ninety grams) measuring 50 mm × 53 mm × 20 mm. What makes this timepiece so sensational is its wonderful open-worked architectural façade encapsulated in dome sapphire crystal that showcases the three-dimensional mechanics of the watch. Beneath the futuristic exterior lies a sophisticated 41-jewel Triple Axis Central Tourbillon hand-winding movement.

Tourbillon Phantom, 1. Switzerland

Vincent Calabrese Tourbillon Phantom

Vincent Calabrese is an avant-garde watchmaker based in the district of Morges, Switzerland. Since 1977, he has developed many complications for other brands like Corum, Bell & Ross, and Blancpain. The Tourbillon Phantom is one of his most accomplished timepieces to date. The watch is small by modern standards and has a diameter measuring 36 mm. What makes this timepiece so amazing is its sublime hand-crafted sapphire crystal case that creates the illusion that the dial and mechanism are suspended in thin air. Other features include 18-karat gold floating lugs and an innovative case back crown system. At the heart of the watch is a refined 17-jewel hand-winding movement.

Timer II, 20. Germany

Vintage VDB Timer II

Vintage VDB is a small boutique watchmaker situated in the city of Erfurt, Germany. Stephan Obst, Helmut Lamberty, and Christian Seidel established the company in 2010. One of their latest models is the stylish and durable Timer II. This watch has a massive solid bronze case measuring 55 mm × 57 mm × 20 mm. What makes this watch so appealing is its distinctive military green dial with contrasting orange markers that gives the timepiece a wonderful retro appearance. Other features include a black anodized aluminum bezel, sporty chronograph sub counters, and a domed sapphire crystal lens. Powering the watch is a Swiss-made 25-jewel Valjoux ETA 7750 mechanical self-winding movement.

V-30/49-01-A, 40. Germany

Vyskocil V-30/49-01-A

Volker Vyskocil is a specialist watchmaker situated in the heart of Nettetal, Germany; from a young age he was passionate about mechanical clocks and watches. This stimulated him to establish his own unique brand, Vyskocil. So far he has only produced one, exciting watch called the V-30/49-01-A. This timepiece has diminutive proportions and a luxurious platinum case measuring 38 mm × 10.5 mm. What makes this watch so delightful is its wonderful hand-decorated matte grey dial that works in perfect harmony with the raised silver indexes. Other features include a small second sub counter and retrograde power reserve indication. Powering the watch is a bespoke mechanical hand-winding movement.

Academy Christophe Colomb Hurricane Grand Voyage II, 10. Switzerland

Zenith Academy Christophe Colomb Hurricane Grand Voyage II

Zenith is widely acknowledged in the world of horology as a watchmaker of distinction. Although the company has historical roots dating to 1865, they are now owned by luxury goods group LVMH (Louis Vuitton, Moët, Hennessy). One of their most exclusive and impressive watches to date is the wonderful Academy Christophe Colomb Hurricane Grand Voyage II. Dimensionally the timepiece is well proportioned and has a 18-karat rose gold case measuring 45 mm × 14.635 mm. What makes this watch so outstanding is its beautiful multi-layered white enamel dial. Other features include a decorative crown and large aperture (encapsulated in dome crystal) displaying the gyroscopic self-regulating gravity control module. Powering the watch is a 53-jewel mechanical hand-winding movement containing 353 individual components.

Cyclone Diamond Edition, 10 diamond 30 gold. Switzerland

ZZ Watches Cyclone Diamond Edition

ZZ Watches is a small independent brand in the heart of Geneva, Switzerland. Married couple Valeria and Cyrus Zeinal-Zade are the creative force behind the company. Probably the most distinctive and exclusive watch they have produced to date is the Cyclone Diamond Edition. This watch exudes modest proportions and has a diameter measuring 39 mm. What makes this timepiece so wonderful is its 18-karat white gold/steel case garnished with (5.02 karats) diamonds, giving the watch an elegant appearance. Interestingly, hours and minutes are displayed via rotating discs (visible through two windows) because the dial is completely devoid of hands. Beneath the luxurious façade lies a modified Swiss-made Soprod A10 25-jewel mechanical self-winding movement.

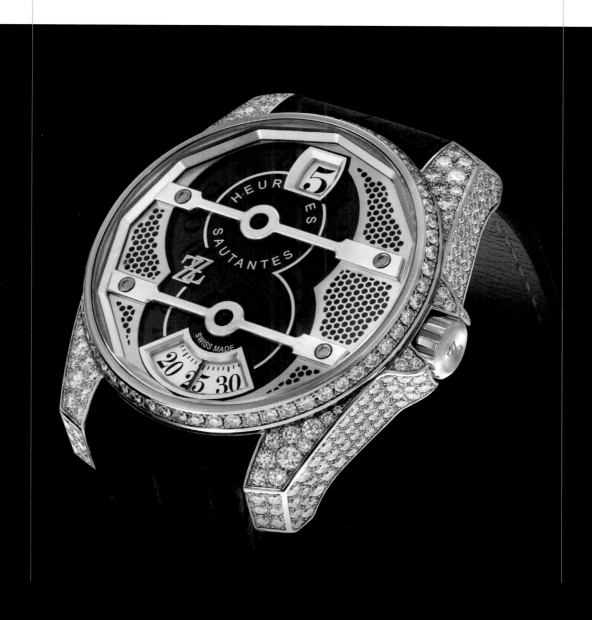